Lying, Misleading, and What Is Said

Lying, Misleading, and What Is Said

An Exploration in Philosophy of Language and in Ethics

Jennifer Mather Saul

OXFORD
UNIVERSITY PRESS

OXFORD
UNIVERSITY PRESS

Great Clarendon Street, Oxford, OX2 6DP,
United Kingdom

Oxford University Press is a department of the University of Oxford.
It furthers the University's objective of excellence in research, scholarship,
and education by publishing worldwide. Oxford is a registered trade mark of
Oxford University Press in the UK and in certain other countries

First Edition published in 2012
Impression: 3

British Library Cataloguing in Publication Data
Data available

Library of Congress Cataloging in Publication Data
Data available

ISBN 978-0-19-960368-8

Printed and bound by CPI Group (UK) Ltd, Croydon, CR0 4YY

I dedicate this book to Ray, Theo, and my parents, Frank and Julie Saul. Without your love and support, I'd just be swearing at the internets.

Preface

The term 'what is said', and other related terms, are currently being used in a huge variety of ways in the philosophy of language. They are the subject of many complicated, ingenious, and passionate debates. One of the subjects of debate is how, and whether, our use of these terms relates to that of ordinary speakers. Are these debates merely a matter of theoreticians arguing about their theoretical vocabulary? Is anything at stake here that ordinary speakers do, or should, care about? The answers to these questions (and many others) seem at this point to be far from clear.

Not all the terms philosophers discuss are like this. Take, for example, terms such as 'lie' and 'mislead'. The distinction between lying and merely misleading is an immensely natural one. It is clearly not a mere philosophers' distinction, unfamiliar to ordinary life and of dubious significance. It is a distinction that ordinary speakers draw extremely readily, and generally care about, and a distinction recognized and accorded great significance in some areas of the law. Interestingly, it is also a distinction that turns on the notion of *saying*: you cannot lie unless you deliberately *say* something false (or at least something you believe to be false).

And this distinction matters. Recently, it played a crucial role in the scandal that nearly led to President Bill Clinton's removal from office. During the scandal (which will be discussed much more extensively in Chapter 5), Clinton made a number of utterances that seemed carefully phrased in order to avoid lying by merely misleading. One famous one was his carefully present-tense denial of a relationship with Monica Lewinsky: "There is no improper relationship."

In fact, the lying–misleading distinction is quite frequently a significant one in politics. Awareness of the lying–misleading distinction underlies the infamous political practice of push-polling. A push-poll is a campaign tactic in which voters receive a phone call purporting to be a genuine poll for the purpose of gathering data. But no data is gathered. Instead, the voter is asked a series of questions which are meant to suggest the truth of some information considered likely to be detrimental to the opponent of the campaign behind the push-polling. One of the most famous examples of this was the push-poll conducted by George W. Bush's

2000 primary campaign against John McCain, in which voters were asked, "Would you be more likely or less likely to vote for John McCain for president if you knew he had fathered an illegitimate black child?" John McCain had not in fact fathered any illegitimate child, black or white. To say that he had done so would have been a lie. But the poll effectively insinuated that he had, without saying it. And this is widely believed to have cost McCain the South Carolina primary.[1]

But it's not just politicians who care about the lying–misleading distinction—nearly all of us seem to. Think of what you might do if you found yourself at the deathbed of a kind old woman wanting to know if her son is all right. You saw him yesterday (at which point he was happy and healthy), but you know that shortly after your meeting he was hit by a truck and killed. If you're like most people, you would consider it better to utter (1) than (2)—because uttering (1) is merely misleading while uttering (2) is a lie. And the reason for this is that what (1) says is true, while what (2) says is false.

(1) I saw him yesterday and he was happy and healthy.
(2) He's happy and healthy.[2]

I have long been interested in what is said, and I have even longer been interested in the careful statements and machinations of politicians. It was natural, then, for me to begin to wonder about the relationship between the notion of saying involved in the very intuitive distinction between lying and misleading and the notions discussed in the philosophy of language literature. If the notion involved in the lying–misleading distinction *is* one of those from the philosophy of language literature, then we know that this notion, at least, is one that ordinary speakers do think and care about. If it is not, then we know that there is a problem to be dealt with: there seems to be a notion of saying that matters to ordinary speakers which, despite the enormous literature on saying and related notions, has not yet been captured. In Chapter 2, I argue that our situation is the latter one. Despite the vast literature on saying, we do not yet have a notion suitable for doing the work needed by the lying–misleading distinction.

One response to this situation might be to pronounce the lying–misleading distinction unworkable or illusory because it does not draw on any currently defended notion of saying. But this seems to me extremely

---

[1] See, for example, http://en.wikipedia.org/wiki/Push_poll
[2] This is loosely based on an example from Williams (2002: 114).

unappealing. We should not give up on such an intuitive and widely accepted distinction without a fight, and there is no reason for confidence that all viable notions of saying have already been put forward. Instead, it seems to me that the right response is to try to develop a notion of saying that can do the work needed for the lying–misleading distinction. This is what I attempt in Chapter 3. There I argue for a notion of saying that can do the work we need for the lying–misleading distinction. (I also sketch out the further work that would need to be done to develop this notion fully.)

All of the discussion in Chapters 1–3 takes as its starting place the thought that there *is* an intuitive distinction between lying and misleading, to which many assign moral significance. But it is worth investigating whether the many are *right* to assign this moral significance to the distinction. After all, morally preferring misleading to lying is really rather puzzling. In both cases, a speaker deliberately attempts to induce a false belief in their audience. Why on earth should it matter whether they do this by *saying* something false or merely conveying it by some other means? Chapter 4 tackles this difficult question. In the end, I argue that there is no across-the-board moral distinction such that any particular act of deception is better if accomplished by mere misleading rather than lying. But I also argue that the lying–misleading distinction may still have moral significance, in that whether a person decides to lie or mislead quite frequently reveals something morally significant about their character.

Although the arguments in Chapter 4 concern the moral significance of the lying–misleading distinction, they draw in part on insights from philosophy of language. Even though it seems quite clear that the lying–misleading distinction involves an intersection of issues in philosophy of language and ethics, there has been relatively little attention paid to this intersection. Discussions of what is said and discussions of the ethics of lying and misleading have proceeded almost totally in isolation from each other. Chapter 5 represents a further chipping away at this divide. In this chapter, I consider a selection of interesting, historically significant or difficult cases for the lying–misleading distinction, working through both the ethical and philosophy of language issues for each one. What we see, in doing this, is that the work on the nature of saying in Chapters 2 and 3 fits rather nicely with the work on the morality of lying and misleading in Chapter 4. Together, I think they serve to provide illuminating analyses of a variety of puzzling and problematic cases. They also serve to show that philosophical reflection on the lying–misleading distinction, and even on what is said, can shed light on significant events and phenomena in the real world.

In case it is not yet apparent, this book is very different from others in philosophy of language. A first difference is that the chapters focussed exclusively on developing a notion of what is said—Chapters 2 and 3—are very different in goal and style from most philosophy of language. They do not aim to show that any theory of saying is *the right theory* (or the wrong theory) of saying. Instead they attempt to discern which is the right theory of saying for a particular purpose—drawing the intuitive distinction between lying and misleading. When I argue that a notion of saying is not suited to this purpose, it is not an argument that the notion is *wrong*. One reason for this unorthodox approach is simply that my topic is the lying–misleading distinction, so my focus is exclusively on that.

Another reason, however, is that I strongly suspect it does not make sense to ask which notion of saying (or, indeed, of related notions such as semantic content) is *right*. Rather, on the view that I am drawn to, it only makes sense to ask which notion of saying is right for a particular purpose. So, for example, one theory might be well suited to an interest in what is consciously represented during the processing of utterances, while another might be well suited to an interest in what gets reported by indirect speech reports. There is no reason at all to expect that these should coincide, nor is there any reason to judge one of these interests more legitimate than another.

I will not, here, attempt to argue that this suspicion of mine is true.[3] Instead, Chapters 2 and 3 can be read as a case study of what results from taking this idea as a working hypothesis. In those chapters, rather trying to find *the* right view of saying, I instead look just for the right view of saying for a particular purpose. I think this methodology yields substantial illumination. If that's right, it might well be worth pursuing with other purposes in mind. It *may* even be more worth pursuing than disputes over which is the *correct* conception. But, as I say, I will not be arguing for that.

Another way in which this book differs from most in philosophy of language is that it is concerned with a distinction of at least apparent normative moral significance. Indeed, although Chapter 4 draws on material from philosophy of language, it is not itself philosophy of language, but

---

[3] I have, however, previously argued that something like this is going on in Grice's and Relevance Theorists' discussions of what is said (Saul 2002).

ethics; and Chapter 1 is in no way philosophy of language. There is nothing at all new about drawing connections between philosophy of language and ethics, in the case of metaethics. Indeed, much of metaethics arguably is a sort of philosophy of language. A few philosophers have recently explored connections between philosophy of language, applied ethics, and normative political philosophy—for example, work by Hornsby, Langton, and others in feminism on free speech, pornography, and silencing.[4] But these projects are concerned with using philosophy of language to shed light on ethical and political issues. This book argues not only that philosophy of language can shed light on topics in ethics, but also that ethics can shed light on philosophy of language. After all, its starting point is the thought that reflecting on a distinction from ethics between lying and misleading can shed light on saying, long a central notion in philosophy of language.

This book, then, steps aside from disputes in philosophy of language over the *right* understanding of saying (or semantic content, or other related notions) and asks different questions. It asks whether there is a notion that can play the role of saying for the intuitive distinction between lying and misleading; whether that distinction actually has the moral significance that so many accord it; and whether drawing together insights from these two discussions can shed light on puzzling and problematic examples. It is, as I've said, a new and somewhat experimental sort of undertaking. It undoubtedly suffers from all the flaws of new and experimental endeavours. My main hope is that, for all its flaws, it may offer a new and fruitful direction for research: one that leads (at least temporarily) away from internecine and increasingly acrimonious disputes in philosophy of language; and one that shows philosophy of language to be both illuminating for and illuminated by reflection on matters of real-world ethical significance. The main goal of this book is not to argue for a particular conception of lying, or of saying, or of the relationship between the two. Instead, it is to demonstrate that it is worthwhile to consider these issues together, and that doing this offers a new and intriguing direction for both those interested in lying and those interested in saying. I also hope, though, that the material in Chapter 5 will show that reflecting on both of these philosophical topics can help us in understanding actual events of genuine human concern.

---

[4] There is also a growing industry discussing racial and other epithets in philosophy of language.

Acknowledgements

I have been working on this book for an embarrassingly long time, and over the course of this time I have discussed it with so many people that I am sure to leave some out. Nevertheless, I owe enormous debts to many people, and I do want to try to thank them.

For discussion of this book and related issues, I am very grateful to Jonathan Adler, Heather Arnold, Kent Bach, David Braun, Chris Bennett, Elisabeth Camp, Josep Corbi, Michael Devitt, Ray Drainville, Nir Eyal, Don Fallis, Paul Faulkner, Michael Glanzberg, Tobies Grimaltos, Sally Haslanger, Daniel Hill, Chris Hookway, Larry Horn, Rosanna Keefe, Jeff King, Simon Kirchin, Charlie Lassiter, James Mahon, Steve Makin, Eliot Michaelson, Nenad Miscevic, Marta Moreno, Carlos Moya, David Owens, Lina Papadaki, François Récanati, Frank Saul, Joe Saul, Julie Saul, Seana Schiffrin, Roy Sorensen, Rob Stainton, Andreas Stokke, William Tweedly, and David Wilmsen. I have also benefited from presenting this book many times over the years—so many that I think I have probably forgotten some. These included the Philosophy Cafe (Leeds), the Focus on the Speaker Panel at the International Pragmatics Research Association (Manchester), Trust and Lying Workshop (Sheffield), the Lying, Saying and Meaning Workshop (Oslo), the Dubrovnik Philosophy of Linguistics Conference, MIT, the universities of Barcelona, Birmingham, Crete, Hull, Rochester, Manchester, Lund, Sheffield, Valencia, Wolverhampton, York, I am especially grateful to my colleagues and students at Sheffield, the best place I have ever encountered to do philosophy. I also thank the AHRC and the Leverhulme trust for their support of this research.

Finally, I thank Ray Drainville for the lovely book cover, which I think I may like even better than the book.

Contents

1

Lying

It is worth noting at the outset that the word 'lie' is used in many ways.[1] On some very broad usages, any deceptive practice, linguistic or not, may count as a lie. So, for instance, a facelift could be seen as a way to lie about one's age. On some slightly less broad usages, any deceptive linguistic utterance is a lie.[2] These usages of the word 'lie' are not the ones that concern us here, as they are very clearly not involved in the distinction between lying and mere misleading. Our concern here will be exclusively with the understanding of 'lie' on which it contrasts with 'mislead'. This clearly requires a much narrower understanding of 'lie'. We'll begin with a couple of classic examples.

Consider again—because I'll return to it repeatedly—Bill Clinton's utterance, (1), made at a time when his relationship with Monica Lewinsky was in the past but nevertheless a present topic of conversation.[3] Assume for the purposes of this book that Clinton's understanding of 'improper relationship' was the same as the ordinary one in English, and that Clinton and Lewinsky did have an improper relationship.

---

[1] In fact, some have argued that the correct way to understand 'lie' is via prototype theory. Coleman and Kay (1981) conclude from their empirical research that statements are judged to be lies or not on the basis of how well they conform to a lie prototype. Their research does not consider the hypothesis that there are distinct usages of 'lie' deserving of separate consideration, and that these distinct usages of the term might have affect the results they obtained. Also, the only choices they offer subjects are 'lie' or 'not lie'. Other categories such as 'deliberately misleading but true' are not offered. If what I argue here is correct, offering this additional choice might have a substantial effect on their results.

[2] Another variant is Jorg Meibauer's definition, which counts both assertions and implicatures believed to be false as lies (2005: 1382). Again, this is a broader understanding than the one I am concerned with here, since—on the understanding I'm concerned with here—implicating is a very important way of merely misleading rather than lying.

[3] This utterance took place during an interview with Jim Lehrer of PBS, on 21 January 1998 (PBS 1998), as the scandal was beginning to break.

(1)   There is no improper relationship.

Initially, many took this as a denial that Clinton had ever had an improper relationship with Monica Lewinsky. But they were wrong: 'is' is a present-tense verb, so Clinton's utterance of (1) was exclusively a present-tense denial. Clinton did not lie in uttering (1), though he did (perhaps deliberately) mislead. And by the end of the day, everyone had noticed how carefully phrased Clinton's utterance was.

But the distinction between lying and merely misleading does not, of course, begin in the Clinton era. Alasdair MacIntyre offers an example from the life of St Athanasius:

Persecutors, dispatched by the emperor Julian, were pursuing [Athanasius] up the Nile. They came on him travelling downstream, failed to recognise him, and enquired of him: "Is Athanasius close at hand?" He replied: "He is not far from here." The persecutors hurried on and Athanasius thus successfully evaded them without telling a lie. (1994: 336)

Although Clinton and Athanasius (probably) both thought they were doing something morally preferable by misleading rather than lying, the moral significance of the distinction between lying and misleading is highly disputable. Some, in fact, would think that Clinton's careful misleading is somehow sneakier and more reprehensible than an outright lie; or that Athanasius did not need to carefully mislead—he would have been equally saintly[4] if he'd lied, given the nature of his situation. Later, in Chapter 4, we will enter into this dispute. All that matters to us now is the fact that all parties to the dispute agree that the distinction between lying and mere misleading *exists*. There are disagreements about its moral significance, but none of the disputants challenge the distinction's existence.

The goal of this chapter is to arrive at a definition of 'lie', used in such a way as to contrast with 'merely mislead'.[5] We will see that the notion of

---

[4] Larry Horn has noted that 'saintly' is not actually the first adjective to spring to mind when one knows a bit more about Athanasius, who apparently didn't balk at engaging in a bit of violence or kidnapping (2010: 331).

[5] The contrast between lying and misleading is actually a little bit more complex than it may initially appear, due to certain facts about misleading: (a) one may mislead accidentally, but one cannot lie accidentally; and (b) for a misleading to occur, the audience must end up with a false belief. In addition, we ordinarily take many lies to also be misleading. The real contrast that interests me is between lying and (intentionally) *merely* misleading. (In fact, in Chapter 4, we will see reason to be even more precise than this.) Sometimes, however, I'll say

saying plays a crucial role in this definition. In the next chapter, we will explore existing conceptions of what is said and related notions, and see that none of them is adequate to this distinction.

The definition of 'lying' I will arrive at in this chapter is the following.

Lying: If the speaker is not the victim of linguistic error/malapropism or using metaphor, hyperbole, or irony, then they lie iff (1) they say that P; (2) they believe P to be false;[6] (3) they take themself to be in a warranting context.

My goal in this chapter is to motivate the above definition, which will be used in the remainder of the book. In the next sections, I will give reasons for formulating the definition as in Lying, contrasting my choices with those made by others who have given definitions of 'lying'.[7]

1 Saying

Some definitions of 'lying' use terms other than 'says'. Chisholm and Feehan (1977), for example, use 'asserts' (151), as does Adler (1997: 437). Carson (2006) opts for 'states'. This is not, however, an interesting difference at all. Among philosophers of language, 'asserts' is just as contentious as 'says' and the two terms are sometimes used interchangeably. Those who write on lying also often use the terms interchangeably (see e.g. Adler 1997: 237; Carson 2006: 284). My decision to use 'says' is really a terminological preference, stemming from my initial and formative immersion in Grice's distinction between saying and implicating. But what I am really after in this book is *whatever* notion plays the variously named role picked out by 'says' in Lying.

'mislead' as a kind of shorthand. These complications regarding misleading are discussed more fully at the start of Chapter 4.

[6] Those who think that lies must be false would rephrase this as "they truly believe P to be false". More on this issue in section 3.

[7] It is worth noting that I don't take this to be the only defensible definition of 'lying' as contrasted with 'misleading'. Indeed, in some of the footnotes I will be paying attention to what happens if one adopts an alternative definition which requires that what is said must be false. The main point of this book, as noted in the preface, is to explore the relationships between lying, misleading, and saying. Different views on how to define 'lying' may lead to different views on how to define 'what is said', and vice versa. So those who make different theoretical choices from mine will get different results. However, I think the choices that I make are well motivated, as described above.

The key role played by 'says' in Lying (and by the related terms in other definitions) is to aid in distinguishing lying from merely misleading. This, as we've noted, is a very intuitive and widely made distinction. Here is another example, of which we'll use a few versions in this chapter.

Suppose that a politician, call him 'Tony', believes that there are no weapons of mass destruction in Iraq, but wants to convince people that there are weapons of mass destruction in Iraq.[8] He therefore utters sentence (2), intending and hoping that he will be believed:

(2)   There are weapons of mass destruction in Iraq.

As it turns out, Tony's belief is right about Iraq: there are no weapons of mass destruction. He is also right about his audience: they are deceived by his utterance into believing that there are weapons of mass destruction in Iraq. Very clearly, Tony has lied.

Now, imagine a slightly different case. Suppose a discussion was taking place about whether or not Iraq had weapons of mass destruction. Tony was asked his opinion, and replied with (3):

(3)   Saddam Hussein is a dangerous man.

Imagine that Tony's audience took him to be conveying that Iraq had weapons of mass destruction, and that this was Tony's intention. In this case, intuitively, Tony did not lie but merely misled. The reason for this would seem to be that what Tony said was true, even though he deliberately conveyed something false.

Without a focus on what is *said*, a definition of 'lying' would run the risk of including all forms of intentional deception. As I've noted, the word 'lie' is sometimes used in just this broad a way. But such broad usages are not our concern here. Our interest is in the strict use of 'lie' that contrasts with 'misleads', and for that, we need to restrict our definition to deception regarding what is *said*. (In fact, we'll see reason to refine this extensively as we go—but this statement is good enough for now.)

2 Must a liar believe what is said to be false?

Thomas Carson (2006) notes that not all dictionary definitions of 'lying' require the liar to believe that what they say is false. Rather, some require

---

[8] As is probably apparent, this example is inspired by Tony Blair and the purported justification for the Iraq war. However, the various 'Tony' examples are wholly fictitious.

that a lie must be 'a false statement made with the intent to deceive'.[9] Call a definition based on this (replacing 'states' with 'says') definition Lying (1).

> Lying (1): A person lies just in case they say something false with intent to deceive.

To see what is wrong with this, consider a new variant of the Tony example above. Imagine again that Tony utters (3), intending to deceive his audience into thinking that Iraq has weapons of mass destruction—but confident that (3) itself is true.

> (3)   Saddam Hussein is a dangerous man.

But imagine that, unknown to Tony, Saddam Hussein has just suffered a stroke that has altered his psyche, rendering him a gentle and kindly soul who is a danger to nobody. According to Lying (1), this is enough to transform Tony's utterance into a lie. But clearly it is not enough. Tony believed himself to be saying something true (despite his intention to use that true statement to induce a false belief in his audience). Tony's utterance is not rendered a lie simply because, unknown to him, what he said was false. What is said must be believed by the liar to be false.[10] Call a definition incorporating both this and our reflections on 'saying' Lying (2).

> Lying (2): A person lies iff they say something false, which they believe to be false, with an intention to deceive.

3 Must what is said be false?

It turns out, however, to be not nearly so clear that saying something false is a necessary condition for lying. Merely *believing* what one says to be false may be sufficient.[11]

---

[9] *Oxford English Dictionary*, quoted in Carson (2006: 286).

[10] Carson, like pretty much all philosophers who have written on the subject, agrees that mere falsehood is insufficient for lying (2006: 286). However, he allows for the possibility of lying by saying something one believes to be *probably false*; or by saying something that one *doesn't believe to be true*. I am suppressing this complication, as (a) I don't think there's a significant difference between believing something to be false and believing it to be probably false; and (b) it seems to me that if one says something that one doesn't believe to be true, but also doesn't believe to be false, this is not a lie. Instead, it's an instance of what Harry Frankfurt calls 'bullshit' (Frankfurt 2005). We'll discuss bullshit at the end of this chapter.

[11] There is some disagreement on this point. Although my view is in accord with Kant's (see Mahon 2003: 112), others including Carson (2006) disagree. If one holds that what is said

To see this, imagine a different version of the Tony example: Tony believes that there are no weapons of mass destruction in Iraq, but wants to convince people that there are. Once more he utters (2):

(2)   There are weapons of mass destruction in Iraq.

This time, however, things turn out differently. Although Tony has no idea of it, there are indeed weapons of mass destruction in Iraq. Despite his deceptive intentions, Tony said something true.

I think intuitions strongly favour the result that Tony still lied—because he took himself to be saying something false. But according to Lying (2), Tony did not lie because what he said was (unknown to him) true. The desire to capture the intuition that Tony lied leads us to reformulate our definition as in Lying (3).

> Lying (3):   A person lies iff they say something which they believe to
> be false, with an intention to deceive.

4 The intention to deceive, and how to phrase it

4.1 In favour of including 'intention to deceive'

Let's consider a definition of 'lying' that does not require an intention to deceive, such as Lying (4).

> Lying (4):   A person lies iff they say something which they believe to
> be false.[12]

Our question now is why we shouldn't define 'lying' as in Lying (4). One way to answer this is to consider the case of metaphors. When we tell jokes, which we often do, what we *say* is often false, and we know this. However, it seems very wrong to describe us as lying in these cases. Imagine, for example, that a friend tells you a joke about

---

in a lie must be false, then there is no reason to move from Lying (2) to Lying (3). I will keep track in footnotes of places where this would matter.

[12] One who believes that lies must be false would reformulate this as:

> Lying (4'):   A person lies iff she says something false which she believes to be false

the number of Bush administration officials it takes to change a light bulb.[13]

It would be absurd to claim that your friend was lying because it doesn't *really* take ten Bush administration officials to change a light bulb. Your friend did, however, knowingly say something false. So why didn't she lie? The answer that leaps to mind is that she didn't intend to deceive you.

4.2 Against simply 'intention to deceive'

If we accept that we must include an intention to deceive, we need to be very careful how we formulate it. If we simply require that there be 'an intention to deceive', we'll get things wrong. The intention needs to be more specific than this. To see this, let's return to Lying (3).

> Lying 3:   A person lies iff they say something which they believe to be false, with an intention to deceive.[14]

Imagine that Beau is a surly misanthrope, and knows this about himself. He wants to deceive people in Sheffield into thinking that he is friendly, and decides to do so by making conversation about the weather. The weather is very cold for Sheffield, although clearly not below 0 C/32 F. Beau utters (4):

---

[13] Here's the joke, if you're interested: How many members of the Bush administration does it take to change a light bulb?

1. one to deny that a light bulb needs to be changed;
2. one to attack the patriotism of anyone who says the light bulb needs to be changed;
3. one to blame Clinton for burning out the light bulb;
4. one to arrange the invasion of a country rumoured to have a secret stockpile of light bulbs;
5. one to give a billion dollar no-bid contract to Halliburton for the new light bulb;
6. one to arrange a photograph of Bush, dressed as a janitor, standing on a step ladder under the banner: Light Bulb Change Accomplished;
7. one administration insider to resign and write a book documenting in detail how Bush was literally in the dark;
8. one to viciously smear no. 7;
9. one surrogate to campaign on TV and at rallies on how George Bush has had a strong light-bulb-changing policy all along;
10. and finally one to confuse Americans about the difference between screwing a light bulb and screwing the country.

[14] Those who think lies must be false would want to reformulate this as:

> Lying (3'):   A person lies iff she says something false, which she believes to be false, with an intention to deceive.

The same objection will apply.

(4)   It's freezing here!

I think it's quite uncontentiously true that Beau has not lied. And yet he has said something he knows to be false, with an intention to deceive. According to Lying (3), then, Beau has lied. But this is clearly wrong. The reason Beau hasn't lied is that what he is intending to deceive his audience about is unrelated to what he said. In order to lie, Beau must intend to deceive them about whether or not it's freezing in Sheffield. This shows us that the deception must be specifically about what is said.

4.3 'Intending audience to believe that P'

The obvious way to incorporate this is to require an intention that the audience believe *what is said* (which the speaker knows/believes to be false). Many theorists require precisely this.[15] Here's one way to do it. I'll start numbering clauses now, as it will serve us well as complexity mounts.

> Lying (4):   A person lies iff (1) they say that P; (2) they believe P to be false; and (3) they intend their audience to believe that P.[16]

5 Against intention to deceive

The overwhelming majority of those who have written on lying require something like Clause (3). But recently this requirement has been subject to quite convincing criticism. Carson (2006), Owens (unpublished), and Sorensen (2007) offer separate excellent examples, which tell against this widespread requirement. These cases are helpfully categorized by Sorensen as "bald-faced lies", lies in which there is no intention whatsoever to deceive.[17] Carson discusses a case of courtroom testimony. Imagine that a man has witnessed a murder, and that there is CCTV footage of him witnessing the murder. The jury has seen this footage and the man knows that the jury has seen this footage. The man is now on the witness stand.

---

[15] See, for example, Chisholm and Feehan (1977) and Adler (1997). Mahon (2008b) takes this to be a feature of standard definitions of 'lying'.

[16] One who thinks lies must be false would need to add a clause stating that P is false. The objections outlined below apply equally well to this version.

[17] An alternative way of handling these cases, suggested by an anonymous referee, is to insist that these are a special sort of case, differing from paradigmatic lies, which do involve an intention to deceive. This seems to me unnecessarily complicated, if we can get a definition that does allow them to be lies. Another alternative is that taken by James Mahon (2008a), who denies that bald-faced lies are lies. Again, I think this is to be avoided if possible.

Because he fears for his life if he admits to having seen the murder, he utters (5).

(5) I did not see the murder.

(5) says something false, the man knows that it is false, and he knows that nobody will believe him. He does not intend to deceive anyone. And yet our view that he has lied on the witness stand is unshaken by the fact that he is not trying to deceive anyone. According to Lying (4), however, he has not lied—because he does not intend his audience to believe him (indeed, he knows that they won't).

Totalitarian states, which both Owens and Sorensen discuss, also offer a rich (though perhaps less clear) source of examples of lying without intent to deceive. One sort of case is much like Carson's witness example—that of show trials in which people are forced to confess to crimes they did not commit. They do not intend to deceive anyone, yet they are forced to incriminate themselves by lying. Since they know they won't be believed, Lying (4) does not count them as lying. Another case is perhaps trickier. This is the case of utterances demanded by a totalitarian state. These utterances of sentences supporting the state are made by people who don't believe them, to people who don't believe them. Everyone knows that false things are being said, and that they are being said only because they are required by the state. There is absolutely no intention to deceive anyone about what is said. In particular, Owens discusses a case raised by Vaclav Havel, of a greengrocer who puts a political slogan in his window in just these circumstances. (If you're worried by the complications raised by examples involving recorded utterances, imagine that the shopkeeper utters the slogan out loud to everyone who comes into his shop.) Havel describes these people as 'living in a lie', and that seems right. Moreover, the specific utterance constituted by the slogan seems to be a lie—even though there is no intention to deceive. Again, Lying (4) would not count these utterances as lies.

I think perhaps intuitions are a little bit less clear about this case than about Carson's frightened witness. It seems somewhat reasonable to suggest that, since everyone is forced to make these false utterances, and everyone knows they are false, they cease to be genuine lies. The reason for this might even be that they cease to have their apparent content, in much the same way that "the dog went to the bathroom" no longer means that the dog went into the room containing the bath.[18] Perhaps they are even treated as meaningless. I think this story is possible, but that something is lost by adopting it wholesale. What is lost is a recognition of the fact that one of the terrible things done by a totalitarian state is to *force people to lie* with these state-supporting utterances. If we treat these utterances as not having their apparent content, we may lose sight of this wrong. On the other hand, treating the utterances as meaningless might be an important sort of resistance, and we would want to acknowledge that. Perhaps the best solution would be one on which we can recognize that in some contexts these will be forced lies and in others they will be meaningless.

What the clearest of these examples show, however, is that—contrary to what almost everyone who has discussed the subject thinks—an intention to deceive is not required for an utterance to count as a lie.

6 Adding 'warrant'

The above examples seem to show that we should not require an intention to deceive for an utterance to count as a lie. But this leaves us with a problem. We included an intention to deceive in our definition, so that we could distinguish cases of lies from cases of jokes. How can we do this if we give up on requiring an intention to deceive? Carson suggests that the key notion we need is one of *warranting*.

If one warrants the truth of a statement, then one promises or guarantees, either explicitly or implicitly, that what one says is true. (2006: 294)

As Carson notes, it is only rarely (for example, in a courtroom) that one explicitly warrants the truth of what one says. But, as he notes, in at least the overwhelming majority of cultures one warrants the truth of what one says unless one is in some special context—e.g. joke-telling—where the warranty is removed.[19] This presumption of warrant is very important.

We can quickly see that warranting has the potential to help us in defining 'lie'. Here's one way of doing this.

---

[18] For more on the process by which idioms like this come about, see Morgan (1978).

[19] For some fascinating examples of cultures that provide exceptions to this, see Brown and Levinson (1987), Wilmsen (2009), and Velleman (2010).

Lying (5): A person lies iff (1) They say that P; (2) They believe P to be false; (3) They say that P in a warranting context.[20]

Carson's frightened witness and the participant in a show trial do not intend to deceive, but it could not be clearer that they warrant the truth of what they say—after all, they have presumably sworn to tell the truth, quite an explicit warrant. Since they know themselves to be saying false things, they lie. Just the result we want. The people living in a totalitarian state, making pro-state utterances, are a trickier case (which they should be). Whether or not their utterances are made in contexts where a warrant of truth is present is not at all clear. In all likelihood, there will be considerable contextual variation. In contexts where the utterances are taken as meaningless, there will not be a warrant of truth. But I think we wouldn't want to take utterances in these contexts to be lies, so our definition does well. In contexts where the utterances are taken more seriously, the warrant of truth may still be present. (Recall that the courtroom examples have already shown us that the warrant of truth may be present even when everyone knows an utterance is a lie.) In these contexts, it feels more appropriate to call the utterances 'lies'. Again, the definition seems successful.

6.1 Knowledge of warranting context

If most contexts are warranting contexts, and only very special contexts are *not* warranting contexts, then sometimes speakers may end up warranting things that they do not intend to warrant. Carson shows this with the case of a person invited both to give a serious address on the state of American politics, and to give a comic one. He gets mixed up about which address he is giving, and recounts a comical false anecdote to the audience for the serious address. Since, unknown to him, the speaker is in a warranting context, he unintentionally warrants the truth of what he says (2006: 296). We would not want to say that this speaker is a liar, but that is what the definition as currently formulated would dictate. We can avoid this consequence with an additional clause, Clause (4).

Lying (6): A person lies iff (1) They say that P; (2) They believe P to be false; (3) They say that P in a warranting context; (4) They do not take themself to be in a non-warranting context.[21]

---

[20] One who believes that lies must be false would add that P must be false.
[21] One who believes that lies must be false would add that P must be false.

But, as Don Fallis (2009) and James Mahon (2008a) have pointed out, this is not yet quite right. The reason is that a speaker might take themself to be in a warranting context when they are not. On Lying (6), this would mean that they are not lying. But this seems wrong. Imagine, for example, that a politician is invited to give a serious address on an issue of great importance, but accidentally finds himself in the wrong room, in a room where the audience is anticipating a fictional monologue about politics (surely there must be an audience for this somewhere!). Because he has been generously paid by lobbyists, our politician plans to lie to his audience about the serious matters of great importance that are his subject. He gives a speech containing a huge number of false claims that he knows to be false, expecting and hoping that he will be believed. But of course he is not believed, and the reason for this is that his audience thinks that he is giving a fictional monologue. Unknown to him, the politician is not in a warranting context. According to Lying (6), this means that the politician is not lying. But that just seems wrong. We can easily fix things—and shorten the definition!—by replacing (3) and (4), above, with (3):

> Lying (7):   A person lies iff (1) They say that P; (2) They believe P to be false; (3) They take themself to be in a warranting context.[22, 23]

7 Final complications

7.1 Metaphors

Consider, the case of Amanda, who utters (6) while being interviewed on *Newsnight*:

> (6)   Tony is a poodle.

Amanda's intention is to convey that Tony is servile and does whatever Bush wants him to do—a popular view of Tony. (And the metaphor she

---

[22] I take Lying (7) to be very similar to Fallis's (2009) definition. The key difference is that Lying (7) uses the notion of a warranting context, while Fallis's uses the notion of a context in which Grice's Maxim of Quality is in effect. I don't think this difference much matters for our purposes. For further discussion of Fallis's definition, see Mahon (2008a).

[23] Carson (2010: 37) responds to Fallis's objection. His response is twofold: he takes the intuitions about Fallis's case to be less clear-cut than they seem to Fallis and to me. But he also notes that he could readily accommodate the case by modifying his definition in a way similar to what I suggest here.

uses is a popular one in the UK.) What she has said, however, is very obviously false, taken literally, as long as Tony is a human being.[24] Moreover, Amanda knows this. And she's very well aware that she's in a warranting context. So according to our current definition, Amanda has lied. But, of course, we don't think that she has—because she was speaking metaphorically. The most obvious way to block this result is by adding another clause, Clause (4).[25] Because irony ("Tony is *such* an independent thinker!") and hyperbole ("Tony is the worst human being ever") pose similar issues, Clause (4) covers them as well.[26] (We will eventually see that this is a problematic way to deal with these cases.)

> Lying (7): A person lies iff (1) They say that P; (2) They believe P to be false; (3) They take themself to be in a warranting context; (4) They are not speaking metaphorically, hyperbolically, or ironically.[27]

7.2 Accidental falsehoods

Sometimes people fail to lie because they have unwittingly said something false. We'll call these cases *accidental falsehoods*, and they will prove important to our discussion throughout the book.

There are several ways that one might accidentally say something false. We have already looked at one such case, in section 2, in which Tony was saying something he *believed* to be true with the intention of deceptively communicating a falsehood. There are also simpler cases. Suppose, for example, that Alfred (like the majority of Americans until recently) believes that Saddam Hussein was responsible for the attacks of September 11th. On the basis of this false belief, Alfred utters (7), below.

---

[24] It's worth noting a complication here. There are some philosophers of language who would take what is said by (4) to be true if Tony does in fact have the poodle traits that are relevant to the metaphorical utterance. This is an additional form of contextual variation permitted by some of those theories of what is said that I call 'Unconstrained' and 'Constrained' in Chapter 2. There we'll see good reasons to reject these theories for the purposes of the lying–misleading distinction, even without looking at the case of metaphor. But I think there are also, quite independently, good reasons to reject this view of metaphor. (These reasons are largely those put forward by Elisabeth Camp (2006).)

[25] Another way to block the result would be to follow Grice's lead (1989: 87) and insist that to say that P one must mean that P. Along with most who have discussed the topic, including devoted Griceans, I think there are good reasons against this. Some of these reasons are the examples I discuss in section 7.2 of this chapter and Chapter 2 of accidentally *saying* something false.

[26] Other figures of speech may need to be added as well, but it should be fairly obvious how to do so.

[27] One who believes that lies must be false would add that P must be false.

(7)   Saddam Hussein was responsible for the attacks of September 11th.

What Alfred said is false. But Alfred does not know this. As a result, Alfred has accidentally said something false—but he has not lied.[28] This case, like the more complex Tony one, is easily accommodated by our current definition of 'lying': Clause (2) is not met in either case, so neither is a lie.

But other cases will force some final modifications to our definition. Another way that someone may accidentally say something false is through uttering the wrong words, due to false beliefs about the words' meaning. A nice example comes from a colleague's time on a post-doc in Mexico. Anna, an English rock climber, wanted to tell her colleagues that many people in England climb without ropes. So she uttered (8):

(8)   En Inglaterra hay mucha gente que escala sin ropa.

(8) actually means that in England there are many people who climb without clothes. This claim is false, but Anna did not lie; she accidentally said something false, through a linguistic error. Our current definition, however, counts Anna's utterance as a lie: she has said[29] that many people in England climb without clothes; she believes this to be false; she knows she's in a warranting context; and she's not speaking non-literally. Our definition, then, is in need of modification. We can capture this case with an additional clause, (5)—though eventually we will see that this, too, is problematic.

> Lying (8):   A person lies iff (1) They say that P; (2) They believe P to be false;[30] (3) They take themself to be in a warranting context; (4) They are not speaking metaphorically, hyperbolically, or ironically; (5) They are not a victim of linguistic error.[31]

---

[28] 'Accidental' may be a somewhat misleading term. There was nothing accidental about the fact that so many Americans had false beliefs about Saddam Hussein—it was carefully engineered. But from these Americans' perspectives, their uttering of falsehoods was accidental: they did not mean to say false things. My use of 'accidental falsehood' is meant to contrast with 'deliberate falsehood'.

[29] There is room for debate here. On Grice's understanding of saying, for example, p must be meant by the speaker in order to be said. See above n. 25.

[30] One who believes that lies must be false would add that P must be false.

[31] I take 'linguistic error' to be a broad enough category to include such people as (a) victims of the Moses Illusion, who respond "Two" to "How many animals of each kind did Moses bring on the ark?"; and (b) the victim of a badgering prosecutor who eventually assents to a sentence so convoluted that he is confused about what he says. Roy Sorensen (2011) discusses cases like these in his 'What Lies behind Misspeaking'.

Cases of malapropism provide a final hurdle for our definition. My favourite non-Bush example comes from my colleague David Bell's neighbour who happily informed him of some home improvement intentions by (inadvertently) uttering (9).

(9) We're having a small conservative built onto the back of our house.

At the moment, our definition counts this as a lie. The neighbour has said she's having a conservative built onto the back of the house; she knows this is false; she knows she's in a warranting context; she's speaking literally; and she's not a victim of linguistic error.[32] But this is easily fixed by altering clause (5):

Lying (8): A person lies iff (1) They say that P; (2) They believe P to be false; (3) They take themself to be in a warranting context; (4) They are not speaking metaphorically, hyperbolically, or ironically; (5) They are not a victim of linguistic error or malapropism.[33]

7.3 Objections, and more modifications

This definition is not without problems, and we will consider a few such problems here. Some of these will force us to another modification of the definition.

7.3.1 Lying with metaphors, linguistic errors, and malapropism?[34] Lying 8, as
formulated above, rules out the possibility of certain sorts of lies—those that make use of metaphors and those that involve linguistic errors and malapropisms. And there are indeed examples like this which may seem, intuitively, to be lies.

Imagine, for instance, that George Bush, knowing full well that Iraq had no weapons of mass destruction, uttered sentence (10), below.

(10) Iraq has weapons of mass production.[35]

---

[32] If one views malapropism as a kind of linguistic error then clause (6) already blocks this case counting as a lie.

[33] One who believes that lies must be false would add that P must be false.

[34] The discussion in this section is very much indebted to discussions with Elisabeth Camp, Don Fallis, Roy Sorensen, and Andreas Stokke, and Andreas's excellent Lying, Saying, and Meaning workshop in Oslo.

[35] This example is based on an actual utterance of Bush's, in which he accidentally substituted "weapons of mass production" for "weapons of mass destruction (text available online at: http://politicalhumor.about.com/library/blbushisms2002.htm).

If Bush actually did know that Iraq had no weapons of mass destruction and did utter sentence (10), we might want to call this a lie. But <u>Lying 8</u> rules this out, by making it a necessary condition for lying that one not misspeak.

Or imagine a native speaker of Spanish who wants to spread the false rumour (in English) that Edna is pregnant. In order to do so, she draws upon her knowledge that 'embarrasada' means pregnant in Spanish and utters sentence (11).

(11)   Edna is embarrassed.

Again, we might want to call this a lie, but <u>Lying 8</u> does not allow us to do so—since our Spanish speaker has made a linguistic error.

Finally, consider the case of a very competitive gardener, who has actually had a bad crop—but who wants to conceal this.[36] She utters (12):

(12)   We've got tomatoes coming out of our ears.

(12) is metaphorical, so it is not eligible to be a lie. And yet, intuitively, we would judge it to be one.

These cases all seem, at least initially, quite worrying. Moreover, as we will see, they are not easily avoided. But after much reflection, I have become convinced that it is genuinely unclear how we should treat these kinds of cases, and that the best definition will be one that avoids passing judgement on them. I explain this below, and then I offer such a definition.

It might seem at first that we could easily avoid these problems by simply dropping clauses (4) and (5), which rule out lying with metaphors, malapropisms, and linguistic errors. This would, of course, pose problems for the cases that motivated these additions. But, worse yet, we still would not get the results that we want.

To see this, consider the case of someone who wants her highly ethical friends to respect her buying habits. She utters (13) by mistake, meaning to utter (13*):

(13)   I always buy free trade coffee.
(13*)   I always buy fair trade coffee.

---

[36] I'm grateful to an anonymous referee for this example.

As a matter of fact, she always does buy free trade coffee rather than fair trade coffee, and she knows this. So the sentence she actually uttered was true, and known by her to be true. That's enough to keep her utterance from being a lie, even if we use a definition of 'lying' that doesn't block lies by malapropism:

Lying (7): A person lies iff (1) They say that P; (2) They believe P to be false; (3) They take themself to be in a warranting context.

Intuitively, though, this case is no different from the Bush case. They each meant to lie and accidentally uttered the wrong sentence. The only difference is that one accidentally uttered sentence turned out to be true and the other false. These cases should, it seems, meet the same fate. So leaving off (4) and (5) would not be a way to solve our problems.

Moreover, I think a plausible case can be made that ruling out lying by malapropism, metaphor, and linguistic error is the right thing to do. We are, after all, concerned with the lying–misleading distinction. It is reasonable to suppose that the inclination to insist that the metaphorical speaker and others are lying comes from forgetting this fact, and focusing just on their deceptiveness. There is, as I've noted, a conception of lying that is much broader than that involved in the lying–misleading distinction, one that counts any deceptive utterance as a lie. On that conception, all of these utterances are lies. But what we're interested in here is lying *as opposed to misleading*, a notion for which what is actually said is crucial. Once we recall this, it no longer seems so clearly problematic to rule out lying via metaphor, malapropism, and linguistic error. Those who deceive in these cases are being just as deceptive as those who lie (in the narrow sense that we're examining), and we may judge them just as harshly morally. But they are arguably not lying, in the narrow sense that is the topic of this book.

In the narrow sense that is the topic of this book, a verdict of lying is far from clearly right in these cases. Once we keep the lying–misleading distinction squarely in focus, it seems far less appealing to say that Bush lied when he declared Iraq to have weapons of mass production. It's perfectly plausible to say that he tried to lie, but in fact spoke so ineptly that he simply failed to make sense. Things are similar with the Spaniard's attempted lie: the speaker was trying to lie, but she simply didn't manage to say what she wanted to say. In both cases, when we are inclined to say the speaker lied, we are focusing on what they tried to do, or alternatively on their deceptiveness. But neither of these is sufficient for lying in the sense that contrasts with misleading. Metaphorical and hyperbolic lies are perhaps a trickier case. Suppose I write in a letter of reference for a student I know to be excellent, "Amanda is basically a turnip" or "Amanda has less philosophical ability than my left shoe". At first glance, it seems hard to resist the conviction that these are lies. But it is not unreasonable to maintain that this is due to my shocking deceptiveness. "You lied when you said she's a turnip", best makes sense as an accusation when we are thinking of lying as general deceptiveness. When we focus on lying as contrasted with misleading, we focus on what is said, and it seems just beside the point to note that *Amanda is a turnip* is false because she's a human being.

Because of these uncertainties, it seems to me that the best definition for our purposes will be one that avoids passing judgement on putative lies involving metaphors, mis-speaking or linguistic error. One way of getting this result is the definition I call 'Lying', below.

Lying: If the speaker is not the victim of linguistic error[37]/malapropism or using metaphor, hyperbole, or irony, then they lie iff (1) they say that P; (2) they believe P to be false;[38] (3) they take themself to be in a warranting context.[39]

This definition does not classify Amanda as a liar for saying "Tony is a poodle"; nor does it classify David Bell's neighbour as a liar for saying that she was having a conservative built onto her house; nor does it classify the rock climber as a liar for saying, in Spanish that many British people climb without clothes. Instead, it avoids judgement on these cases. Similarly, it avoids judgement on cases such as my malicious letter saying that Amanda is basically a turnip; or Bush's claims about weapons of mass production. It avoids judgement about these cases because it does not purport to be a fully complete definition of 'lying'. It is, instead, a definition of 'lying' for cases that do not involve malapropism, linguistic error, metaphor,

---

[37] It is far from clear that all cases of linguistic error pose problems for a definition of 'lying' in the way that the ones we have discussed do. It seems unlikely, for example, that errors regarding verb agreement would do so. However, it is harmless for our purposes if the category of utterances on which our judgement fails to pass judgement is a little bigger than it needs to be.

[38] Those who think that lies must be false would rephrase this as "they truly believe P to be false".

[39] I am grateful to Rosanna Keefe for her help in thinking through these issues.

hyperbole, or irony. This means, of course, that there is still work to be done—ideally, we would like a definition that passes judgement on these cases as well, and in a way that accords with our intuitions. But this must remain a task for another time. For the purposes of this book, however, this definition is sufficient: none of the cases that will be crucial to our discussion involve malapropism, linguistic error, metaphor, hyperbole, or irony.

7.3.2 Taking oneself to be in a warranting context Clause (3) of our definition of 'lying' requires that the speaker take themself to be in a warranting context. But, of course, they are very unlikely to think to themself, "this is a warranting context". Does this mean that the definition of lying will almost never be satisfied? No. The belief that one is in a warranting context is overwhelmingly likely to be a tacit, inexplicit belief. Any plausible view on mental states will countenance tacit beliefs, as they are a ubiquitous feature of our lives. (We tacitly believe that there's ground under our feet, that gravity works the same way in every room that we enter, and that an elephant is bigger than a cockroach, even if we never explicitly consider these propositions.) A speaker who takes it for granted that they are in the sort of context where sincerity is expected (that she's not, e.g. in a play or telling a joke) is a speaker who takes herself to be in a warranting context. There is no requirement at all that she needs to consciously formulate and reflect on this belief.

7.4 Summing up

This definition, Lying, is the one that we will work with throughout this book.

> Lying (8):   If the speaker is not the victim of linguistic error/malapropism or using metaphor, hyperbole, or irony, then they lie iff (1) they say that P; (2) they believe P to be false;[40] (3) they take themself to be in a warranting context.

I do not take myself to have established that it is the only possible definition of 'lying' as contrasted with misleading, but rather to have shown its plausibility and given some reasons for adopting it. The task for the next two chapters is to work out what conception of saying can do

---

[40] One who believes that lies must be false would add that P must be false.

the work needed for this definition. Obviously, if different definitions of 'lying' were adopted, a different conception of saying might be called for; and I cannot explore all of these options.[41] My main goal, however, is to demonstrate the intricate way that these issues fit together. And Lying— which is a very plausible and well-motivated definition[42]—will serve this purpose well.

7.5 Coda: a contrast with bullshit

Lying, as we understand it here, is distinct from bullshitting, brilliantly analysed by Harry Frankfurt (2005).[43] Bullshitting is closely related to lying. The main contrast is that bullshitters really don't care at all about truth: "the motive guiding and controlling [his speech] is unconcerned with how the things about which he speaks truly are" (Frankfurt 2005: 55). The liar says something that they take to be false, while the bullshitter does not care about truth. Consider, for example, Tony's utterance of (2):

(2)   There are weapons of mass destruction in Iraq.

Suppose that Tony had no idea whether or not there were weapons of mass destruction in Iraq. He uttered (2) because he thought that doing so would be a good way of achieving his goals. Truth simply didn't come into Tony's calculations about what to say. If this is the case, then Tony's utterance of (2) was bullshit.[44]

---

[41] See Mahon (2008b) for a very comprehensive and useful taxonomy of definitions of 'lying'.

[42] Or so it seems to me.

[43] His short book, *On Bullshit*, was originally a paper. But during the Bush era it was reissued as a book and became a bestseller.

[44] Roy Sorensen (2011) develops a different conception of bullshit, and also allows for lies in which the speaker is simply unconcerned with truth value. On Sorensen's understanding of lying, a speaker lies just in case they assert S without believing that S is true. (S is a sentence or something resembling a sentence, which Sorensen calls a 'pseudo-sentence'.) 'Believing' is to be understood here as what Sorensen calls 'shallow belief'. He does not define 'shallow belief', but it seems to be *something like* a disposition to assent to S. This is a very different sort of definition of lying, which may offer a way out of problems raised later for various conceptions of saying. However, I think it faces its own difficulties. In particular, it would seem to count metaphorical utterances as lies, and—perhaps most importantly—it depends on a notion of shallow belief that seems to me to need more spelling out. (Disposition to assent isn't quite right: Sorensen argues that the person who mis-speaks doesn't lie because they shallow-believe the sentence that they utter. But they might well not assent to that sentence when uttered by somebody else.) Carson (2010: 58–64) also disagrees with Frankfurt's account. It seems to me that Carson's disagreements stem from quite a different use of 'bullshit' from the one that Frankfurt is analysing.

2

The Problem of What Is Said

This chapter examines the relationship between theoreticians' notions of what is said (and the like) and the ordinary, intuitive distinction between lying and misleading. We will see that, despite the huge proliferation of conceptions of what is said (and related notions) in the literature, *none* of these notions can capture the intuitions that we have about the lying–misleading distinction. The main conclusion of this chapter, then, is that there is a problem to be solved. The next chapter will attempt to sketch out a way that it might be solved.

1 Background and stage-setting

Although there has been relatively little attention to the lying–misleading distinction by philosophers of language and linguists,[1] there has been a great deal of attention to the concept of what is said. Most contemporary discussion takes as its starting point H. P. Grice's immensely intuitive distinction between what is said and what is implicated. We will do so as well.

1.1 Grice on what is said

Grice was the first philosopher to systematically distinguish between *what is said* and what is otherwise communicated, and to tell a compelling story

---

[1] There are some exceptions to this. Rob Stainton explicitly connects the topics in his 2006. I discuss his views towards the end of this chapter. And the linguist Larry Horn (2010) uses examples of lying and misleading to argue against Relevance Theorists' claims that an Austere conception of saying must be useless. Horn's discussion is fascinating, but it does not tackle the details of various sorts of non-Austere conceptions of saying (e.g. Constrained versus Unconstrained), nor does he offer details of his favoured Austere notion of saying. Michaelson (unpublished ms) develops ways (different from those I develop here) to use definitions of 'lying' as a test for semantic content. Finally, Elisabeth Camp (2006: 207–8) uses examples involving the lying–misleading distinction to argue that a notion of *what is strictly speaking said* is very important to our everyday practices.

about how at least some of what is otherwise communicated comes to be communicated. Our focus will, of course, be on what is said. Grice does not offer a beautifully clear definition of what is said, instead preferring to draw attention to this concept by way of an example:

A and B are talking abut a mutual friend, C, who is now working in a bank. A asks B how C is getting on in his job, and B replies, *Oh quite well, I think; he likes his colleagues, and he hasn't been to prison yet.* (Grice 1989: 24)

B's reply clearly suggests something beyond the bare fact that C hasn't been to prison—perhaps that C is likely to be dishonest, or that C's colleagues are likely to frame him. (Which of these is suggested will depend enormously on the specific facts known in the context.) And yet, equally clearly, it *says* none of this. Grice goes on to explain further that he is assuming "to a considerable extent an intuitive understanding of the meaning of *say* in such contexts" (1989: 24–5). He does, however, specify that he means "what someone has said to be closely related to the conventional meaning of the words (the sentence) he has uttered" (1989: 25). That which B's reply suggests is what Grice calls a 'conversational implicature'. It is, roughly, what the audience needs to assume the speaker to believe in order to understand the speaker as cooperative.[2]

Through Grice's discussions of what is said (and the contrasting notions that he developed), some things become clear.

1. What is said is very closely linked to the sentence uttered, and varies very little from one context to another (unlike what is conversationally implicated).
2. What is said by a sentence containing an ambiguous word such as 'bank' can vary from one context to another.
3. An utterance's truth value is determined by what is said.[3] Moreover, if something is not relevant to this truth value, it is not a part of what is said, even if it is a part of the meaning of the sentence uttered. Grice considers the example "He is an Englishman; he is, therefore, brave" (1989: 25). Because the meaning of 'therefore' does not affect

---

[2] For much more on the definition of 'conversational implicature', see (for example) Davis (1998), Saul (2001, 2002, 2010).

[3] I am not actually sure that it makes sense to talk about the truth value of an utterance, but for now this simplification is useful.

the truth value of the utterance, it is not a part of what is said. (For Grice, it is a conventional implicature.)

This is, initially, a tremendously appealing picture, and one that fits well with our reflections so far on lying and misleading.[4] If I respond to the dying woman with, "I saw your son yesterday and he was happy and healthy", the fact that the son is dead at the time of my utterance does not make my utterance false. The claim that her son is still alive was not a part of what is said, so it's not relevant to the truth value of my utterance. And we can be very confident of this, because what is said is closely linked to the sentence I uttered, and that sentence didn't contain any words such as 'alive' or 'dead'. It is, instead, a conversational implicature: in order to understand me as being cooperative (in this case, giving her the information that she has requested), the woman needs to understand me to believe that her son is still alive.

1.2 Complications

But, as subsequent philosophers and linguists have discovered, there are some very important—and ubiquitous—sorts of cases that Grice simply doesn't discuss. And most of them don't fit at all easily into his picture. Before we get to these, though, let's briefly turn our attention to one sort of case that does fit relatively easily into Grice's framework: that of the so-called 'pure indexicals'.

1.2.1 Indexicals Grice doesn't discuss terms such as 'I', 'here', and 'now' in much detail. These are terms whose reference varies with context, but for which that reference is completely determined in each context by a linguistic rule (such as 'I' refers to the speaker).[5] However, it seems

---

[4] Grice also requires that what is said must be meant. But subsequent Griceans have not followed him with regard to this rather unintuitive requirement. It seems extremely natural to describe a mis-speaker as saying something that they don't mean. But on Grice's own view, this would be wrong: something is not said unless it is meant. Grice himself deals with cases where a speaker does not mean what their words express by saying that the speaker only *makes as if to say* what the words express, a very awkward formulation. For reasons like this (but not limited to this), most theorists have found Grice's requirement of meaning to be over-restrictive.

[5] Actually, there are some quite difficult complications having to do with recorded utterances and the like, but we'll ignore them here, as we'll have plenty of complications to deal with anyway. (For more on these, see, Predelli (1998, 2002), Corazza, Fish, and Gorvett (2002), Romdenh-Romluc (2002, 2006), Atkin (2006).)

overwhelmingly likely that he would treat them in much the same way that he treats ambiguous terms, allowing what is said by sentences containing them to vary with context. This is necessary for such very commonplace utterances to have truth values, since truth value is determined by what is said. This fits well and easily into the picture sketched above. We can simply add that context will determine the contribution that pure indexicals make to what is said, as well as selecting meaning for ambiguous terms.

1.2.2 Demonstratives Far more problematic are the genuinely demonstrative terms, such as 'this', 'that', 'she', and 'he'. Any utterance of a sentence containing one of these words will require contextual supplementation for the word to refer, and in order to have a truth value. And it is far from clear how this contextual supplementation will work. (Is the referent what the speaker is pointing at? What she thinks she's pointing at? What if she's not pointing? Is it what she intends to refer to? What the audience takes her to refer to? What it's reasonable for the audience to take her to refer to?)[6] What is very clear, though, is that contextual supplementation is needed beyond that involved in disambiguating or in supplying a reference for a fully rule-governed indexical such as 'I'. Grice did not discuss reference determination for these terms at all, although he did use examples involving these terms, clearly assuming that the terms did contribute to what is said. Take, for example, the sentence 'He is an Englishman; he is, therefore, brave' (1989: 25). Grice uses this sentence to illustrate conventional implicature, arguing that the connection between Englishness and bravery is not a part of what is said. In so doing, he notes in passing that "I have said that he is an Englishman". This is important: Grice clearly does not take there to be anything strange about saying something by using a demonstrative such as 'he'. It's clear Grice does take an utterance of a term such as this to contribute its reference to what is said. Nonetheless, the difficulty posed by these terms for a Gricean theorist has left them a point of some contention: although most assume that they must somehow contribute to what is said, we'll see later in this chapter that Kent Bach denies this.

---

⁶ See, for example, Wettstein 1984, Reimer (1991a, b), Bach (1992), and (for an overview) Braun (2008). See also the discussion in Chapter 5, section 2.3.

1.2.3 Completion Other sorts of constructions are even trickier. Take, for example, an utterance of (1):

(1) Amanda is ready.

Context will select a particular Amanda as the reference for 'Amanda'. Neither 'is' nor 'ready' is a pure indexical. Nor are they ambiguous. There is, then, no room on the picture we have seen so far for any contextual contribution to what is said other than a reference for 'Amanda'. But without some further contextual contribution, (1) does not seem to say anything truth evaluable. (What is Amanda ready for? Another fruity cocktail? A swim in the pool? A job interview?) But on Grice's view, what is said is meant to be determine truth value, and we would normally take an utterance of a sentence such as (1) to have a truth value. Moreover, we use sentences like this all the time.

(2) Beau is late. (*For his wedding? For Happy Hour? Sending in his tax form?*)
(3) Charla's had enough. (*To drink? To eat? Of the sun?*)

To get a truth value for an utterance of a sentence such as (1), we need some contribution from context *beyond* those called for by the obvious indexical terms. These cases are the ones that Kent Bach calls Completion (1994) cases, and we'll do so too.

1.2.4 Expansion Now consider sentence (4):

(4) Billy went to the top of the Empire State Building and jumped.

Assuming the reference for 'Billy' is fixed by the context, there are no further ways for context to make a contribution to what is said by an utterance of (4), on the Gricean picture. But if we take what is said to be determined simply by the meanings of the words in (4), and we take that to determine truth value (as the traditional Gricean would), it turns out that an utterance of (4) will be true even if Billy simply bounces up and down, or practises the high jump. Many take this to be highly counterintuitive and insist that (4) must, in a normal context, say something that is true only if Billy jumped off the edge of the Empire State Building. To get this result, one must allow some further contribution from context, beyond what Grice would. (It needs to be contextual because there are many contexts in which a use of 'jumped' conveys no such thing, and even some contexts in which a use of (4) wouldn't convey this.) And there are many similar cases. An utterance of (5), for Grice, would be true even if the marriage followed the birth of the children. And an utterance (6) would be true if the speaker had had breakfast only once in her life, ten years previously.

(5)   Amanda and Beau got married and had children.
(6)   I've had breakfast.

These cases are the ones that Bach (1994) calls Expansion cases, and we'll also do so.

1.3 Dealing with the complications

As I noted earlier, Grice did not consider the sorts of cases described in the section above. We don't know what he would have said about them if he had done so. Consideration of these sorts of cases has led to a huge proliferation of views on what is said, as well as a huge proliferation of technical notions related to what is said. One key point of disagreement (though not described in these terms) has been whether to take as primary Grice's view that what is said should be tightly linked to the sentence uttered, or whether to take as primary the idea that it should be the bearer of truth conditions. Views that take the former as primary will in general allow much less contextual variation than views that take the latter as primary. But even this is a gross oversimplification, due to the fact that (a) some theorists take the sentence uttered to contain a large number of 'hidden' elements that are not obvious from its surface form, and which allow for a great deal of contextual variation closely linked to the sentence; and (b) pretty much every theorist uses different technical vocabulary. Many of these disagreements are not relevant to our concerns here, so I will try to avoid these as far as possible.

My goal here is to explore what conception of what is said is needed for for the lying–misleading distinction. This conception of what is said will be the one called for by the definition of 'lying' we arrived at in the last chapter. According to that definition, lying turns crucially on what is said.

Lying: If the speaker is not the victim of linguistic error/malapropism or using metaphor, hyperbole, or irony, then they lie iff (1) they say that P; (2) they believe P to be false;[7] (3) they take themself to be in a warranting context.

---

[7] Those who think that lies must be false would rephrase this as "they truly believe P to be false".

This project is a very different one from the usual ones concerning what is said (and related notions). This has some important consequences. One is that nothing I say here should be taken as an *objection* to any of the views discussed. These views were not proposed as ways of capturing the lying–misleading distinction. In fact, as noted in the preface, I suspect that different notions of what is said may be needed for different purposes (both theoretical and ordinary). That a notion fails for one purpose by no means counts against its usefulness for another. The other important consequence is that the project here calls for a new taxonomy of views. I will divide views on what is said into three broad categories, according to how much contextual variation these views allow. The views I am discussing will be *based on* ones from the literature.[8] What I'll be doing is testing notions of what is said—based on views of semantic content, what is said, explicature, impliciture, and assertion—to see how these views fare with regard to the lying–misleading distinction. We will see that none of them succeeds.

1.4 Terminology

I will be introducing my own terminology for categories of views, in part because the meanings of more familiar terms, like 'contextualist' and 'minimalist' is so disputed,[9] but also because I want to divide up the conceptual territory in a somewhat novel way. My discussion will begin with the loosest, most contextualist understandings of what is said. I will call these 'unconstrained' understandings of what is said. On these understandings, what is said by a speaker who utters a sentence S need not include anything corresponding to the overt constituents of S. Next, I will look at what I call 'constrained' understandings of what is said. These are views on which what is said must include constituents corresponding to the overt constituents of the sentence uttered, but substantially expanded by contextual[10] contributions. Finally, I will turn to what I call 'austere'

---

[8] It is important to emphasize that these views are only based on ones in the literature. Many of the views in the literature are ones that their authors would object to calling views on what is said. In addition, most (if not all) would deny that they are views about whatever it is that fulfils the role of what is said for the lying–misleading distinction.

[9] For a good discussion of this disputed vocabulary, see Borg (2007).

[10] Even the use of the word 'contextual' here is contentious. Kent Bach restricts the use of the word in the narrow manner that I describe later.

conceptions of what is said, which allow for only very minimal contextual involvement.[11]

1.5 Accidental falsehood

I have already mentioned the notion of accidental falsehood. When we are trying to decide whether someone is lying, we might say "no" because they have merely misled: what they said was true, and they knew this. We might also say "no" for a different reason: although what they said was false, they believed it to be true.[12] As I noted in the last chapter, I call this sort of case 'accidentally saying something false'. What I wish to note here is that it seems clear that the same notion of what is said is involved in both the judgement that someone has lied and the judgement that they have not lied but merely *accidentally* said something false. Thus, judgements about accidentally saying something false will also help us in figuring out what notion of what is said we need for the lying–misleading distinction. In fact, we really have a three-way distinction—between lying, misleading, and accidentally saying something false. Often, for convenience, I will refer to the lying–misleading distinction. But when accidental falsehood is relevant I will mention it as well.

2 Unconstrained conceptions of what is said

One important fact about whatever conception of what is said is involved in the lying–misleading–accidental falsehood distinction is that it is very clearly something intuitively accessible to speakers.[13] Ordinary speakers have no difficulty drawing these distinctions, which suggests that the notions they turn on must be very intuitive. It seems to many that the most intuitive notions of what is said are the loosest, most contextual ones. This idea suggests that we should begin our search by examining a very loose, contextualist notion of what is said. With that in mind, I start with what I call an Unconstrained conception of what is said.

---

[11] Apologies for adding to the quantity of jargon in the world.

[12] There are also, of course, lots of other reasons: e.g. the person sincerely said something true, and did not mislead in any way.

[13] Accessible in the sense that they are able to employ it in rendering judgements about what is said; not in the sense that they are able to produce a definition of it.

Unconstrained Theorists are very impressed by the wide range of things that may be communicated by an utterance of a sentence. What is communicated will vary enormously from context to context in extremely unpredictable ways, and Unconstrained Theorists aim to do justice to this fact. An Unconstrained conception of what is said is very loose, allowing what is said to deviate radically from the sentence uttered. Indeed, as noted above, what is said need not even include constituents corresponding to constituents of the sentence uttered. Cappelen and Lepore's (2005) Speech Act Pluralism about what is said is a view of this sort.[14] We'll see that we can rather quickly set aside such conceptions for the purposes of the lying–misleading distinction. For this distinction, we need what is said to be much more closely related to sentence meaning.

By way of illustration, we will examine the notion of what is said involved in Cappelen and Lepore's Speech Act Pluralism, "No one thing is said (or asserted, or claimed, or...) by any utterance: rather, indefinitely many propositions are said, asserted, claimed, stated, etc" (199). They give no particular formula for working out which propositions are said by an utterance. Instead, they seem to allow that if a reasonable person might claim that something is said by an utterance, then it is—even if it is quite distant from the words uttered. For example, they discuss O. J. Simpson's utterance, "At 11.05 PM I put on a white shirt, a blue Yohji Yamamoto suit, dark socks, and my Bruno Magli shoes" (196). Cappelen and Lepore offer several possible true reports of what OJ said. Among them is "He said that he stopped exposing himself to the neighbours right after 11 PM (said in a context where it is common knowledge that he was standing naked in front of the window before 11 PM)" (196).

A person lies just in case the following holds:

Lying: If the speaker is not the victim of linguistic error/malapropism or using metaphor, hyperbole, or irony, then they lie iff (1) they say that P; (2) they believe P to be false;[15] (3) they take themself to be in a warranting context.

---

[14] John Searle's (1978) and Charles Travis's (1996) views also fall into this category. In their case, it is due to a rejection of the idea that the words in a sentence might have meanings which could provide such constituents of what is said.

[15] Those who think that lies must be false would rephrase this as "they truly believe P to be false".

On the Unconstrained view described above, any utterance will say many things. So, if we use this for the lying–misleading distinction, a person will count as lying just in case she takes one of these things to be false and the other conditions are met. This view makes it very easy to lie, and indeed very hard not to do so (at least if one is trying to mislead). We can see this quickly and easily from a look back at our initial examples.

Although Clinton will have said something true when he uttered sentence (7), he will also have said something false.

(7)   There is no improper relationship.

We know for a fact that some would report this utterance with "Clinton said there was never an improper relationship", since they did so. And this is indeed reasonable, using a loose understanding of 'say' and bearing in mind that the context was one in which a possible past relationship was being discussed. According to Cappelen and Lepore, then, he will have said that there never was an improper relationship. Call this falsehood P. In order to have lied, Clinton must have believed that P was false, which he surely did. Clauses (1) and (2) are met, then. He knew himself to be in a warranting context, and he did not take himself to be speaking metaphorically. Nor was he a victim of linguistic error or malapropism. So the rest of the definition is satisfied. The same will be true with the carefully crafted sentence, "I saw your son yesterday, and he was happy and healthy". After all, the old woman might report this with a relieved "she said my son is fine", and this is what the speaker intends—despite the speaker's knowledge that her son is not fine at all. So this utterance too is a lie. And of course Athanasius lied. All the most careful efforts to avoid lying (while still misleading) turn out to fail. And whatever the morality of these efforts, we do think that they succeed in misleading rather than lying.

This conception of what is said, then, is clearly not what we want for the lying–misleading distinction. More generally, Unconstrained conceptions of what is said seem especially poorly suited to this distinction: intuitively, the sort of what is said involved in the distinction will be one that is very closely tied to linguistic meaning. I have no doubt that proponents of these conceptions would agree: they did not propose them to deal with the lying–misleading distinction, and they are quite clearly ill-suited to it.[16]

---

[16] It's worth noting that Soames's 'what is asserted', as described in his 2002 and 2010 fares somewhat differently. For Soames (2010: 163), p "counts as asserted . . . only if p is an obvious,

3 Constrained conceptions of what is said

The natural next move is to turn to a somewhat stricter notion of what is said, one that is tied more closely to the sentence uttered. Many theorists have offered such notions (often as accompaniments to stricter and/or looser notions), under a variety of names. What all these proposed notions have in common is that what is said must be in some way crucially linked to the structure of the sentence uttered. More specifically, one necessary condition for saying that P by uttering S will be that P includes constituents corresponding to all the overt constituents of S. Put metaphorically, the overt structure of the sentence uttered gives us at least a skeleton on which what is said is hung. These theories allow additional material to be added by the processes I call "completion" and "expansion" below.[17] I will call a conception like this a "Constrained" conception of what is said. A Constrained conception of what is said is what we arrive at if we use any of the following notions as our notion of what is said: Relevance Theorists' explicature (Sperber and Wilson (1986/1995); Carston (1991, 2002)); Bach's impliciture (1994); King, Stanley, and Szabo's semantic content/what is said (Stanley (2000, 2002, 2005); Stanley and Szabo (2002); King and Stanley (2005)); Recanati's (1989, 2001) What is said; Stainton's (2006) what is said; Taylor's (2001) semantic content; and what Soames calls the 'enriched proposition' in his (2010).[18] (Some of these theorists would strongly oppose calling

relevant and a priori consequence of the enriched proposition(s) asserted . . . in uttering p . . . together with background presuppositions at the time of use (which . . . must be shared by conversational participants)." Let's consider the case of misleading the old woman. It seems likely that *my son is alive and well* is an obvious, relevant, a priori consequence of what I have said, together with the background assumptions that the old woman is making. However, these background assumptions (e.g. that the speaker is trying to give her a relevant answer to her question) are not actually shared, since the speaker knows some of them to be false. Soames's view, then, does not fall prey to this problem. However, what is asserted for him *does* include what he calls the "enriched proposition". Any conception of saying which includes this will suffer from the problems outlined in the next section.

[17] It is crucial to my understanding of Constrained conceptions that they allow both of these processes. If one adopts a definition of 'constrained conception' that does not have this feature, then my own preferred view, laid out in Chapter 3, will qualify. Nothing really hangs on these terminological choices.

[18] I recognize that (to put it mildly) these theorists would not normally be categorized together. There are important differences between them, but these are not my focus here. It is also worth noting that it is, as far as I can tell, impossible to find neutral terminology that is acceptable to all. Even the word 'context' is open to dispute, as noted above (see n. 10). I am using it in a broad sense, which is at odds with Kent Bach's much narrower usage (which I discuss later in the chapter)

their notions 'what is said'. But recall that I'm simply looking for a notion to do the work of what is said for the lying–misleading distinction. This notion may legitimately be based on a notion that is not named 'what is said'.)

This sort of conception of what is said looks initially to have very good prospects of doing what we need for the lying–misleading distinction. As we saw in the last section (and as we might have suspected), in order to draw this distinction we need what is said to be tied to sentence meaning. However, the literature is by now filled with examples purporting to show that our intuitions demand a notion of what is said which allows substantial contextual contributions beyond those obviously called for by the sentence. Since the lying–misleading distinction is an intuitive one, surely we must then need a notion that allows this sort of contextual supplementation. We will see, however, that there are real problems for this idea.

3.1 Completion

On a Constrained conception of what is said, what is said involves very important contextual contributions that go beyond the obvious constituents of the sentence uttered. One sort of contextual contribution is what we have already called *completion*. The details of what goes on in such cases are a matter of controversy. But common to all understandings is the thought that some sentences not containing standardly accepted indexical terms require contextual supplementation in order to express complete, truth-evaluable propositions.

Given the right context, Constrained Theories would claim that utterances of the unstarred sentences below say what would typically be said by utterances of the starred sentences—or any of a wide variety of other options.

> (1) Amanda is ready.
> (1*) Amanda is ready for another fruity cocktail/her job interview/a swim in the pool.
> (2) Beau is late.
> (2*) Beau is late for his wedding/for Happy Hour/submitting his taxes.
> (3) Charla's had enough to drink/to eat/of the sun.

3.2 Expansion

Another sort of contextual contribution is what we have already called *expansion*. Depending on the theorist, what goes on in Expansion gets described in different ways.[19] But the basic idea is that, without contextual supplementation beyond that called for by standardly accepted indexical terms, the utterance would express a proposition that the speaker doesn't mean and/or the audience doesn't grasp. In order to get a proposition that's meant/grasped, contextual supplementation is needed.

For example, typical utterances of each of the unstarred sentences below are taken to say what would typically be said by utterances of the starred sentences.

(4)   Billy went to the top of the Empire State Building and jumped.
(4*) Billy went to the top of the Empire State Building and jumped off the edge of the building.
(5)   Amanda and Beau got married and had children.
(5*) Amanda and Beau got married and then had children.
(6)   I've had breakfast.
(6*) I've had breakfast today.

3.3 Accidental falsehood

The first set of problems we will examine for this view concern the notion of accidentally saying something false. We will explore these difficulties by considering three versions of the same example.

3.3.1 Billy and the Empire State Building, Version 1   Imagine that I watch Billy go to the top of the Empire State Building and jump up and down three times. Returning from my day I recount what I saw, by uttering (4)—not realizing how my audience will interpret me.

(4)   Billy went to the top of the Empire State Building and jumped.

My audience, Fred, interprets me as claiming that Billy jumped off the edge of the building. This claim would of course be false. Have I lied? Clearly not. Quite obviously, I did not deliberately say anything false. Have I, then, accidentally said something false? Again, clearly not. It is,

---

[19] One difference is that some do not call the process that they are endorsing 'expansion'. For Jason Stanley, for example, all of the contextually supplied constituents are called for by elements of the sentence uttered—but, crucially some of these elements are non-overt. On this view, what takes place would more properly be called 'completion'. My focus, however, is on whether or not the contextually supplied elements are called for by *overt* constituents of the sentence uttered. Hence I can treat Stanley's account as, for my limited purposes, like that of those who endorse Expansion.

quite simply, true that Billy went to the top of the Empire State Building and jumped. The fact that Fred interpreted me as saying more than this has no bearing on what I said. Intuitively, then, my utterance was true but misleading: I neither lied nor accidentally said something false.

According to Constrained Theories, this cannot be the case if my utterance of (4) is a typical one. For Constrained Theorists hold that typical utterances of (4) say what (4*) does. If we take my utterance to be a typical one, then, I have said something false. I did not realize I was saying something false, on this view, so I did not lie. Constrained Theorists must maintain, however, that I nonetheless accidentally said something false.

How might a Constrained Theorist block this verdict? The answer is simple: by maintaining that, in some way, my utterance was not a typical one. The obvious candidate is the fact that I neither intended nor expected my utterance to be interpreted in the way that it was. This idea offers us a few possible necessary conditions for what is said that might do the needed work:

(Sp1)   In order to say that P, the speaker must intend to communicate that P.[20]

(Sp2)   In order to say that P, the speaker must expect to communicate that P.

(Sp3)   In order to say that P, the speaker must have a conscious representation of P.

There is, however, a clear potential problem that arises if any of these is adopted as a necessary condition for what is said: one of our initial examples of accidentally saying something false turns out not be an example of this at all. We can no longer maintain that Anna said that many people climb without clothes in England, as she neither intended nor expected to communicate this, and she had no conscious representation of this.

But perhaps this sort of case isn't so worrying. We can simply maintain that standard intuitions are wrong about cases like these—such cases are, after all, abnormal in involving linguistic error. It seems quite reasonable to treat linguistic error as a special case, and not worry about getting the "wrong" results for such cases. Even if we do this, however, problems will remain.

---

[20] Rob Stainton would endorse this condition, and would insist that a speaker cannot intend something that they do not think the audience can reasonably be expected to understand (2006: 224). This qualification does not have any impact on the examples I discuss.

3.3.2 Billy, Version 2 Imagine another, slightly different, incident: I watch Billy go to the top of the Empire State Building, walk to the edge, and jump into the air. Appalled, I turn and run away, thinking that I have just watched Billy throw himself off the top of the Empire State Building. I tell Ginger my story, by uttering (4).

(4) Billy went to the top of the Empire State Building and jumped.

By this, I mean that Billy threw himself off the edge of the building—it does not occur to me to think that he might not have done so. Ginger, however, knows that Billy is a performance artist, rehearsing a piece that involves much bouncing up and down on the top of the Empire State Building. In addition, she wrongly believes that I am aware of this. Ginger, then, assumes that what I mean does not in any way include the idea of jumping off the building. As it turns out, Ginger's supposition about Billy's activities is correct.

If all this is right, what I said was true—even though Billy did not jump off the top of the building as I thought he would. Some evidence for this comes from the fact that when I learn the truth I will not take myself to have learned that I have accidentally said something false. Instead, I'll think that what I said was true. Moreover, I have not even misled anyone. Despite my own false belief, what I said was true and non-misleading.

In order to get the result that I did not say that Billy jumped off the edge of the building, Constrained Theorists must have some reason to rule my utterance a non-typical one. For if it is a typical one, they must maintain that I have said the same thing that one would say by uttering (4*):

(4*) Billy went to the top of the Empire State Building and jumped off the edge of the building.

An utterance of (4*) would be false, albeit accidentally. But we have seen that intuitively my utterance of (4) is true—and not even misleading.

The reason for judging my utterance to be a non-typical one cannot be one of the speaker-oriented necessary conditions for what is said that we have considered. All of these conditions were met: I *meant* that Billy jumped off the building's edge, I consciously represented this claim, and I expected to communicate it. In this scenario, the elements that might block the conclusion that I have said this are on the audience's side: Ginger did not take me to have meant what (4*) expresses. Moreover, it would not have been reasonable—given her background beliefs—for Ginger to take me to have meant this.

Possible necessary conditions for saying:

(Aud1)   In order for an utterance to say that P, its audience must take the speaker to mean that P.

(Aud2)   In order for an utterance to say that P, it must be reasonable for its audience to take it to take the speaker to mean that P.

(Aud3)   In order for an utterance to say that P, its audience must *reasonably* take the speaker to mean that P. [This condition simply combines the first two.]

We have now seen reasons for Constrained Theorists to include both speaker-oriented and audience-oriented necessary conditions for saying that P. Suppose that they do so. It turns out that, no matter what combination of conditions (Sp1)–(Sp3) and (Aud1)–(Aud3) they require, problems remain.

3.3.3 Billy, Version 3   Imagine that my perspective on the incident is just as it was in the previous example: I falsely believe that Billy jumped off the edge of the building the top of the Empire State Building. I tell my story to Harry, again by uttering (4).

(4)   Billy went to the top of the Empire State Building and jumped.

Harry, however, is in the same epistemic position as I am, so he takes me to mean something like (4*).

(4*)   Billy went to the top of the Empire State Building and jumped off the edge of the building.

Eventually, both Harry and I learn that Billy was only practising his performance art, and that he simply bounced up and down on the building's edge. What will we conclude about my utterance? It seems to me very clear that we will not take me to have said something accidentally false. Instead, we will realize that what I said was true, albeit in a surprising way. Intuitively, my utterance was true but (unintentionally) misleading.

None of the necessary conditions for saying that we have considered on the behalf of the Constrained Theorist can block this result. After all, I mean to communicate what's said by (4*), I represent it to myself, and I expect to communicate it. Harry—quite reasonably—takes me to mean what's said by (4*). All of the conditions we have considered are met, and yet it does not seem that I have said what's said by (4*). In order to get this result, a Constrained Theory would need find some new reason to rule my utterance a non-typical one.

3.4 Lying

A Constrained conception of what is said also goes wrong when it comes to the distinction between lying and misleading. This can be seen fairly readily by considering one of the classic examples from the literature and what we have learned in the discussion above.

Consider a fairly standard Expansion example, (5).[21]

(5)   Amanda and Beau got married and had children.

According to Constrained Theorists, an utterance of (5) will typically say what (5*) expresses:

(5*)   Amanda and Beau got married and then had children.

Now imagine a case in which I am reporting on Amanda and Beau to Amanda's rich fundamentalist uncle. He is considering leaving his fortune to Amanda, but he will only do so if Amanda has been leading a wholesome, traditional life. As it happens, Amanda and Beau had two children out of wedlock and only later got married. I want Amanda to get her uncle's money, but I don't want to lie to him. So I utter (5), knowing that he will interpret my utterance as meaning that the marriage preceded the children. I'm right, and he does so.

Intuitively—whatever we may think of my morality—I have succeeded in misleading Amanda's uncle without lying to him. But Constrained Theories seem unable to obtain this result. To see this, recall our definitions of 'lying'.

---

[21] Bach discusses the closely related "Jill got married and became pregnant", a typical utterance of which he takes to carry the conversational impliciture *Jill got married and then became pregnant* on pp. 19–20 of his 2001. Carston makes it very clear that she takes temporal order to be a part of the explicature in examples such as this (Carston 1991: 40–1; Carston 2002: ch. 3). Similarly, although King and Stanley (2005: 156–9) postulate a different mechanism from Carston's, they take temporal order to be a part of the semantic content of an utterance of a sentence such as (5).

> Lying: If the speaker is not the victim of linguistic error/malapropism
> or using metaphor, hyperbole, or irony, then they lie iff (1)
> they say that P; (2) they believe P to be false;[22] (3) they take
> themself to be in a warranting context.

On Constrained Theories, as long as my utterance of (5) is a typical one I have *said* that the marriage preceded the children. This is false and I know it's false, so (1) and (2) are satisfied. Moreover, I'm very clearly in a warranting context, and I know this. I am also speaking literally, and a victim neither of linguistic error nor malapropism. So, (3), (4), (5), and (6) are also satisfied. I have, therefore, lied. And this seems clearly the wrong result.

To avoid this result, a Constrained Theory would need to claim that my utterance of (5) was in the relevant sense atypical. But it is hard to see how this result can be obtained. None of the necessary conditions we have so far considered will give it to us: I mean what (5*) expresses, Amy's uncle understands me as meaning what (5*) expresses, and it is reasonable for him to do so. Unless there is some other reason that my utterance might be ruled atypical—and I can't really see what this might be—I will have said that the marriage preceded the children. And I will therefore have lied.

So a Constrained conception of what is said is not what we want for the lying–misleading distinction.

4 Austere conceptions of what is said

First, we saw that very loose conceptions of what is said could not do the work that we needed for the lying–misleading distinction. In the last section, we examined Constrained conceptions of what is said, which are more closely linked to the sentence uttered, but which still allow quite substantial contextual contributions. These, too, turned out not to be what we wanted. At this point, the natural next move is to look at conceptions of what is said that are *very* tightly linked to the sentence uttered. What is said, in this sense, is often called 'semantic content', although that term is also used for some Constrained conceptions. The notions discussed in this section are inspired by Bach's semantic content/what is said; Borg's (2004) semantic content, Soames's (2002,

---

[22] Those who think that lies must be false would rephrase this as "they truly believe P to be false".

2005, 2010) semantic content, and Cappelen and Lepore's (2005) semantic content.[23]

'Tightly linked to the sentence uttered' can be interpreted in a variety of ways, and there are a variety of Austere conceptions of what is said that we will examine. What these conceptions have in common is that they allow only very minimal contextual contributions. They do not, then, allow processes of Completion or Expansion to play a role in determining what is said. They differ, however, in many ways. Our particular concerns here will be (a) how they deal with demonstrative reference; (b) how they deal with the cases that others treat as Completion; and (c) how they deal with terms such as 'tall', which most others treat as having content that changes with context.

Because Completion and Expansion cannot contribute to what is said on these views, we get the right verdicts about all the examples discussed in section 6. In all the examples involving Billy and the Empire State Building, all that I *say* is that Billy went to the top of the building and jumped—the claim that Billy jumped off the edge of the building never makes it into what is said. And, as we have already seen, that is just what intuitions dictate about these examples. And when I carefully deceived Amanda's uncle by uttering (5), I misled him but did not lie.

(5)   Amanda and Beau got married and had children.

Again, this is just what our intuitions dictate. An Austere conception of what is said, then, allows us to give the right verdict about these cases. However, we will see that such views still fail to give us what we need in order to correctly draw the lying–misleading distinction.

We will examine three Austere conceptions of what is said: Kent Bach's semantic content/what is said, Emma Borg's semantic content, and Herman Cappelen and Ernie Lepore's semantic content. In keeping with my practice throughout this chapter, I will call all of these notions of what is said. (Borg and Cappelen and Lepore would strongly disagree with this usage.)

---

[23] It is unclear to me where to place Elisabeth Camp's (2006) conception of what is said. It is clearly not an Unconstrained one. But she expresses uncertainty about whether or not to include what she calls 'enrichment' in what is said (307). If she does, hers is a Constrained conception. If she does not, it is an Austere one.

4.1 Bach's semantic content/what is said

In section 1.4, I noted that Grice does not consider cases of Expansion and Completion, and does not discuss demonstratives in any detail. Moreover, I noted that what he says about what is said can be seen to pull in two different directions on these matters: if what is said is thought of primarily as tightly linked to the sentence uttered, then there is not much room for contextual supplementation. But then we will get some rather unintuitive truth conditions. If what is said is primarily thought of as the bearer of truth conditions, on the other hand, we will feel pulled to allow more contextual supplementation. Bach opts strongly and decisively for the first option.

According to Bach—who is in part quoting Grice—what is said by a speaker who utters a sentence "must correspond to 'the elements of [the sentence], their order, and their syntactic character'" (2001: 15). Moreover, "if any element of the content of an utterance, i.e., of what the speaker intends to convey, does not correspond to any element of the sentence being uttered, it is not part of what is said" (Bach 2001: 15). Context is allowed a role on Bach's conception of what is said, but the role is a limited one. For Bach, context only includes things such as location, time, and speaker. It most definitely does not include anything having to do with mental states of conversational participants—such as the speakers' intentions or interests, or the audience's interpretation. So these factors cannot play any role in determining what is said.

On this understanding, what is said is sometimes—perhaps often—so minimal that it fails to be a complete proposition.

This happens with Completion examples such as (1) and (2).

(1)   Amanda is ready.
(2)   Beau is late.

It also happens when demonstratives are used. Indexical terms whose reference is not fixed by context in Bach's limited sense contribute nothing to what is said by speakers who utter sentences containing them.

Consider, for example, an utterance of (8).

(8)   I want to eat that.

For Bach, 'I' refers utterly unproblematically—its referent is wholly determined by one of the elements of context (speaker). 'That', however, is a different matter. There is no rule that will fix a referent for 'that', given a context. The demonstrative 'that' in (8)—or in any sentence—contributes nothing to what is said. All uses of sentences containing demonstratives will fail to say anything truth evaluable, since all such sentences will express partial propositions that contain gaps that need to be filled in order to arrive at something truth evaluable.

4.1.1 Problems

4.1.1.1 DEMONSTRATIVES

One very important place for the lying–misleading distinction is in the courtroom. And one very important sort of courtroom utterance involves identifications of people and objects. Consider the following sentences:

(9) That is not my blood-stained letter opener.
(10) That is the man I saw leaving the scene of the crime.

If perjury law is to be of much use, it must be possible to lie by uttering (9) or (10).[24] We need to be able to say that what is said by one who utters (9) or (10) is something that can be true or false. If we cannot do this, it is impossible for someone to lie by uttering (9) or (10). But this result is just what we get if we use Bach's what is said in drawing the lying–misleading distinction. After all, there is no proposition that the speaker has said. And the thing that the speaker has said is not something that the speaker takes to be false: it seems very odd to suppose that one might take {} is not my blood-stained letter opener to be false.[25]

---

[24] I'm assuming for simplicity an understanding of perjury in terms of lying. In fact, perjury law is often formulated in terms of a wilful statement of a falsehood. Obviously, however, the same notion of what is said is at stake ('statement of something false' can be rephrased as 'saying something false'). I'm grateful to James Mahon for pointing out this complexity.

[25] One might try to resist this result, by allowing that P might not be propositional, and then insisting that one can believe a non-proposition to be false. One would do this, perhaps, by believing that the sentence expressing the non-proposition is false. So, one might believe {} is not my blood-stained letter opener to be false simply because one takes the sentence "that's not my blood-stained letter opener" to be false. However, this solution is not without its own problems. Suppose this view is right. Now imagine that the defendant is confronted with an array of blood-stained letter openers, one of which is his and the rest of which are not. If taking the sentence "that's not my blood-stained letter opener" to be false and uttering it is sufficient for lying (combined with the other clauses of the definition), then the defendant lies with every one of his utterances of these sentences. Even if this problem can be somehow avoided, though, the others noted above are not susceptible to such a solution. It's worth noting that this problem is especially unavoidable for those who hold that lies must be false. For someone holding this view, what is said by a lie simply *must* be false, and therefore must be propositional.

Moreover, we think it is possible for one utterance of (9) to say something true and another to say something false. This is straightforwardly impossible on Bach's view, as neither one says anything truth evaluable. My sincere utterance of (9) is perfectly on a par, as far as truth goes, with the letter opener-wielding murderer's insincere utterance of (9). And that is clearly wrong.

For a further worry, let's alter the example a little. Suppose that the murderer had actually borrowed the letter opener from a friend thirty years before and failed to return it. Technically, it was not his letter opener. Yet in the context it would be very misleading for him to say "That's not my letter-opener". Intuitively, such an utterance would not be a lie—and indeed would be true. But "I've never seen that letter-opener before" would be both a lie and false. On a view based on Bach's, both utterances would have exactly the same truth value—neither would be true. Clearly, we would want to assign different truth values to these utterances, yet we cannot do so.

4.1.1.2 COMPLETION

Bach's view on Completion cases also yields some unintuitive results. Recall that Bach takes nothing truth evaluable to be said in any of these cases. If, intuitively, it is possible to lie with a sentence in need of Completion, then Bach's view violates our intuitions about lying. A case can be made that this is so.

To see this problem, think again about Clinton's utterance of sentence (7).

(7)   There is no improper relationship.

Intuitively, Clinton chose his words carefully, in such a way as to produce a true but misleading utterance. But now notice that (7) is in need of Completion: until it is supplemented in some way, no particular improper relationship is specified. According to Bach, then, (7) says nothing truth evaluable. If we adopt Bach's conception of what is said for the lying–misleading distinction, then, Clinton simply couldn't lie with an utterance of (7), as no proposition which Clinton believed to be false would be said.[26] And the same thing is true for an utterance of (7*).

(7*)   There was no improper relationship.

---

[26] Though see n. 25 for a possible way out of this, and a potential problem for this approach.

If this is right, then Clinton needn't have chosen his words so carefully. Both utterances are completely on a par, as far as truth goes: neither one has any truth value whatsoever. But it seems just wrong to maintain that Clinton's utterance of the carefully worded (7) was no more truthful than an utterance of the past-tense denial in (7*) would have been.[27]

Looking at demonstratives and at Completion cases, then, is enough to show us that Bach's what is said is not what we want to fulfil the role of what is said in the lying–misleading distinction.

4.2 Borg's semantic content

Emma Borg's notion of semantic content yields a version of what is said (though she would not use this term) which is not quite so austere, and therefore much closer to what we seem to need for the lying–misleading distinction. The key differences, for our purposes, between Borg's view and Bach's, are that (a) Borg takes the sentences involved in the cases we have called 'completion' examples to semantically express complete propositions without any contextual supplementation; and (b) Borg allows demonstrative reference to be a part of what is said (in her terms, semantic content).

Borg insists that sentences such as (1) and (3), which others take to be in need of Completion, have no such need.

(1)   Amanda is ready.
(3)   Charla's had enough.

Instead, she claims that they semantically express complete, existentially generalized propositions. (1) expresses the proposition that Amanda is ready for something, and (3) the proposition that Charla's had enough of something. Utterances of these sentences, then, are extremely likely to be true.

Borg fares far better than Bach with the courtroom demonstrative utterances. A speaker who utters (9) or (10) may (in our terminology) say things that are true or false.

(9)   That's not my blood-stained letter opener.
(10)   That is the man I saw leaving the scene of the crime.

---

[27] Once more, the problems are even clearer for those who think lies must be false: there is simply no room at all for any utterance of a sentence in need of Completion to be a lie, since such a sentence can never be used to say something with any truth value at all.

If we use this conception of what is said, then, it is possible to lie by uttering sentences such as (9) and (10), and this is the result that we want.[28]

4.2.1 Problems Borg's view of semantic content is not, however, a wholly appealing candidate for the role of what is said in the lying–misleading distinction.[29]

4.2.1.1 "COMPLETION"
One problem is that of sentences requiring what we have been calling 'completion'. Once more, we can see this problem by considering Clinton's utterance of (7).

(7) There is no improper relationship.

Intuitively, (7) is a carefully worded denial—designed to say something true but misleading. And, intuitively, this effort succeeded: Clinton did say something true but misleading. But if we adopt Borg's semantic content for the role of what is said in the lying–misleading distinction, then this cannot be right: what (7) says is the denial that there are any improper relationships at all, anywhere. This is surely, and obviously, false. Clinton did not, then, succeed in saying something true. (Since Clinton probably did not take himself to be denying the existence of any improper relationships, anywhere, he did not deliberately say something false, so he did not lie.) This seems wrong.

4.3 Cappelen and Lepore's semantic content

Herman Cappelen and Ernie Lepore agree with Emma Borg that the referents of demonstratives make a contribution to semantic content. So far, so good: if we use a notion of what is said based on Cappelen and Lepore's semantic content, we can capture the intuition that it is possible to lie with a demonstrative. They also agree that "completion" cases are

---

[28] It's worth noting, however, that it is actually very tricky for Borg to tell a consistent and clear story about how demonstrative reference is determined, given her Austere notion of semantic content. There are good reasons for Bach's even more austere view, despite its difficulties for our project here.

[29] Borg is well aware that her view would be unintuitive as a view on what is said. That is why she insists that it is a view on semantic content, which she does not take to be something about which ordinary speakers have intuitions. I am testing it here to see if it could fulfil the role of what is said for the lying–misleading distinction. I am sure she would be quite happy with my conclusion that it cannot.

not really in need of Completion, and that sentences containing expressions such as 'tall' semantically express complete propositions that do not vary with context. However, they disagree about "completion" cases. For Borg, as we've seen, (3) is true just in case there's something of which Charla has had enough.

(3) Charla's had enough.

For Cappelen and Lepore, (3) is true just in case Charla's had enough. Cappelen and Lepore insist, with Borg and against Bach, that (3) on its own expresses a complete proposition. But whereas it is easy to see what complete proposition Borg takes (3) to express, it is somewhat more puzzling what the complete proposition *that Charla's had enough* is.

Despite its puzzling nature, however, we *can* see that Cappelen and Lepore's view of semantic content is not what we want to play the role of what is said for the lying–misleading distinction.

4.3.1 Problems Many (myself included) are somewhat puzzled by the idea of a complete, truth-evaluable proposition *that Fred's had enough*. It is not at all clear when this proposition is true or false. But what is very clear is that there is no contextual variation in the content of 'tall', and no additional material to supplement 'enough'. And this is enough to show us that this notion of semantic content is ill-suited to the work we need done for the lying–misleading distinction.

4.3.1.2 COMPLETION

Let's return again to Clinton's utterance of (7).

(7) There is no improper relationship.

Intuitively, as we've noted, Clinton managed to say something misleading but true. If, however, he had used the past-tense verb, he would have lied. Now, imagine that the same facts in the world are true, except that (7) is uttered by Joe Bloggs in a discussion about whether he is having an affair with his colleague Jane Smith (which he is). Intuitively, what Joe Bloggs said when he uttered (7) was false, and Joe has lied. If we use Cappelen and Lepore's semantic content as our notion of what is said, however, (7) says *exactly the same thing* in both contexts, and must have exactly the same truth value. If (7) says something false in Bloggs's context, it says something false in Clinton's. If this is the case, then our intuition about Clinton is wrong: Clinton did not manage to say something misleading but true. If (7) says something true in Clinton's context, it says something true in Bloggs's. Now, Bloggs might still count as lying even if he says something true—because he thought he was saying something false. But if this is the case, then it turns out Bloggs could have avoided lying simply by having a bit more semantic knowledge: if he'd known what he was saying, he would have realized it was true but misleading, and that he had no need to lie. And this, again, seems very wrong.[30]

So Cappelen and Lepore's semantic content is not what we want to fulfil the role of what is said, either.

4.4 Syntactic ellipsis: minimizing the problems for Austere notions of what is said

As it turns out, Austere notions of what is said are not *quite* as unpromising for the lying–misleading–accidental falsehood distinction as they first appear. Recognizing syntactic ellipsis can help with some problem cases. Here is a general explication of syntactic ellipsis, from Rob Stainton (97–8), though really the notion is best made clear by way of example.

I will say that a linguistic expression *r* is *grammatically elliptical* if and only if there exists another linguistic representation *r'* in the language such that *r'* has a longer phonological form than *r* but *r'* has precisely the same context-invariant content as *r*... In syntactic ellipsis, the sound is abbreviated *vis-à-vis* the content that attaches to the type (that what the existence of a "longer" phonological form gets us); nevertheless, the hearer can recover the complete message because the abbreviated sound somehow linguistically encodes the "longer" message (that's what the shared invariant content provides).

To illustrate, let's start with an uncontroversial example of syntactic ellipsis:

(13)   Has Bill gone?
(14)   Yes, he has.

(13) would generally be taken to be syntactically elliptical for (13E):

(13E)   Yes, he has gone

The material in (13E) is explicitly given in the immediately preceding linguistic context. As a result, it is at the level of syntax *really* a part of (13).

---

[30] This example applies just as well to the version of lying that requires what is said to be false.

An austere theorists can accept this sort of claim, and that such material may therefore be a part of semantic content (in our terms here, what is said).

4.4.1 Syntactic ellipsis and Completion If an utterance of (7) is made in the right linguistic context, it may, then, say (semantically express) more than we have thus far supposed.

(7)   There is no improper relationship.

With that in mind, we will examine two possible contexts for Clinton's utterance of (7).

4.4.1.1 THE INTERVIEW

In this context, Clinton's utterance occurs in an interview. The interviewer asks, "Was there ever an improper relationship between you and Miss Lewinsky?" and Clinton responds with (7).

(7)   There is no improper relationship.

Here there is linguistic material present in the preceding utterance that allows syntactic ellipsis to take place. It seems perfectly plausible to maintain that (7) is syntactically elliptical for (7E):

(7E)   There is no improper relationship between me and Miss Lewinsky.

This would allow Austere Theorists to maintain that Clinton said what (7E) says, and therefore that Clinton's utterance was true (instead of being falsified by the existence of some improper relationship somewhere between some individuals). Clinton did succeed in his effort to truthfully mislead.

4.4.1.2 THE OUTBURST

Clinton has not been asked any particular question. Instead, he opens the White House door and shouts at the throng of reporters, "There is no improper relationship!". In this context, there is no preceding linguistic material available to complete (7) by specifying a particular relationship. So, in this context, Clinton's utterance does not say anything specifying a particular relationship. Which unintuitive thing is said will vary by theory, in the ways we have already seen. This seems to me not nearly so problematic as it would be in the *interview* case. In fact, I suspect that without a clear surrounding linguistic context—the sort that would support a syntactic ellipsis story—intuitions are far from clear about whether or not Clinton managed to truthfully mislead, with no linguistic context to fix a particular relationship as the one referred to.

4.4.2 The limitations of syntactic ellipsis Syntactic ellipsis, at least as I have described it, is a limited solution. It does indeed help Austere theories to give plausible verdicts in Completion cases. The Completion cases in which syntactic ellipsis is not possible seem likely to be rather murky ones, intuitively, for the lying–misleading distinction.

More problematic, though, are the Completion cases that fall in between "interview" and "outburst". One key feature of "outburst" was that there was very little stage-setting, linguistic or otherwise, for Clinton's outburst. But now imagine a hospital room. Dave is lying in bed, and two nurses are discussing the treatment he needs. Ed holds up a bottle of heart medicine, points at it, and utters (15):

(15) Has Dave had enough?

Fred replies with (16):

(16) Dave's had enough.

As it turns out, Fred hates Dave, wants him to die, and plans to bring this about by denying him his much-needed heart medicine. When he uttered (16), Fred meant (16*), which he knew to be false.

(16*) Dave's had enough heart medicine.

Intuitively, Fred's utterance of (16) is a lie. But there is no immediately preceding *linguistic* material available to fill in what is needed for Fred's utterance of (16) to say something false. Syntactic ellipsis, as we have so far understood it, cannot help us.

Finally, Rob Stainton (2006: 58) has offered what seems to me a convincing and difficult case of lying. A used-car salesman begins a conversation with a customer by pointing to the odometer on a car and uttering (17):

(17) Driven only 10,000 kilometers.

The salesman knows that the car was actually driven 110,000 kilometres, and that the odometer had reset itself after the first 100,000. Stainton rightly points out that the salesman has clearly lied. Yet there is no immediately preceding linguistic context that can provide material for syntactic ellipsis.

4.4.3 A more expansive understanding of syntactic ellipsis? Jason Stanley (2000) has a much more expansive understanding of syntactic ellipsis. He maintains that syntactic ellipsis does *not* require the use of linguistic material explicitly given in the preceding context. For him, salience is sufficient, and syntactic ellipsis may take place even where there is *no* preceding linguistic material of any kind. He considers a case in which a group of friends are bungee-jumping, and everyone except John has already jumped. Knowing John's fear of heights, Sarah utters (18):

(18) John won't.

Stanley claims that the context is sufficient to raise the expressing 'bungee-jump' to saliency, and that as a result (18) is syntactically elliptical for (18*):

(18*) John won't bungee-jump.

If this is right, then Ed's pointing at the bottle of heart medicine is certainly sufficient to raise 'heart medicine' to salience, and thereby to render (16) syntactically elliptical for (16*) in the example above:

(16) Dave's had enough.
(16*) Dave's had enough heart medicine.

This view, then, seems like it might allow us to uphold the intuition that Fred lied when he uttered (16).

Rey Elugardo and Rob Stainton (2004: 458–9) have persuasively argued that this view of syntactic ellipsis is untenable. The problem is that syntactic ellipsis requires that *specific expressions* be raised to salience, and—despite appearances—this is not the case in Stanley's example, or in mine. To see this, turn first to Stanley. Is there any reason that (18) should be taken as elliptical for (18*) rather than (18**) or (18***)?

(18) John won't.
(18*) John won't bungee-jump.
(18**) John won't jump.
(18***) John won't do it.

Without the word 'bungee-jump' in a preceding utterance, there is no reason at all to prefer (18*) to (18**) or (18***). Since syntactic ellipsis requires *specific expressions*, then, it really cannot work without a preceding linguistic utterance.

Similarly, with my murderous nurse example, there is no reason at all to claim that (16) is syntactically elliptical for (16*) rather than (16**).

    (16)   Dave's had enough.
   (16*)   Dave's had enough heart medicine.
  (16**)   Dave's had enough of that.

The same is true for Stainton's (17).

    (17)   Driven only 10,000 kilometers.

(17) could be elliptical for (17*) or (17**):

   (17*)   This car was driven for only 10,000 kilometers.
  (17**)   This one was driven for only 10,000 kilometers.

It seems, then, that syntactic ellipsis is not really available as an explanation of these cases.

Where are we, then? We have seen that no notion that fits into one of the three categories so far discussed can fulfil the role of what is said for the lying–misleading distinction. Unconstrained notions of what is said simply do not allow for this sort of distinction. Constrained ones yield very unintuitive verdicts—branding as liars people who are mere misleaders, and classifying truths as accidental falsehoods, to name a few. (All of these cases involved Expansion.) Austere theories suffer from a variety of flaws. Some liars do not count as liars, and some careful misleaders who go out of their way to truthfully mislead turn out to have said obviously false things, or nothing at all. And these problems remain, even when we acknowledge and take seriously the possibility of syntactic ellipsis. Since all the conceptions of what is said (and related notions) in the literature seem to fit into these three categories, and since the lying–misleading distinction is one we should at least *try* to preserve, this shows an important gap in the literature. In the next chapter, we will see what sort of notion of what is said *is* called for by the lying–misleading distinction.

3

What Is Said

So far, we have seen that no views of saying (or related notions) in the current philosophy of language literature can do the work that we need done for the lying–misleading distinction. A logical first step towards finding a conception of saying that fulfils our needs is to ask what has gone wrong with the conceptions we've already seen. The short and uninteresting answer as to what has gone wrong with them is that they were not formulated with the lying–misleading distinction in mind. But we can get something a little more interesting out of this if we look at what they were formulated to do. That will be the task of the first part of this chapter. Next, we'll turn to the task of providing an account of what is said that avoids these problems.

1 Diagnosis

1.1 Unconstrained conceptions

We'll begin with the Unconstrained conceptions of saying. Cappelen and Lepore write that the methodology behind their "Speech Act Pluralism" is to "take our nontheoretic beliefs and intuitions about what speakers say, assert, claim, etc. at face value (unless given overwhelming motivation to do otherwise)" (2005: 191). Since it is unquestionably true that the word 'say' has some very broad usages as well as the stricter one involved in the lying–misleading distinction, any conception which simply categorizes all of these usages as saying is going to go wrong when it comes to the lying–misleading distinction. That distinction, as we have seen, turns on a strict notion of saying. To get this distinction right, we need a notion of saying which rules out the broader ones. With an Unconstrained conception of saying, we have seen, pretty much all cases of misleading will count as lies. To see this, it suffices to note that whenever a speaker deliberately misleads their audience into thinking that P it will be reasonable (employing a broad usage of 'say') to describe the speaker as having said that P. If P is false and the speaker knows it, this utterance will count as a lie. As we saw in the last chapter, this means (for example) that Clinton lied rather than misled when he uttered (1).

1.2 Constrained conceptions of saying

Constrained conceptions of saying (as I have called them) come out of a wide variety of background concerns, and form parts of very different outlooks on the nature of communication. All of them, however, are undermined by considering cases of very skilful misleading.

1.2.1 Récanati's what is said and Relevance Theorists' explicature These notions are a part of their authors' efforts to capture psychological reality— that is, to make sense of what actually goes on in audiences' (and sometimes speakers') heads during the uttering and processing of utterances. If something isn't consciously represented by the audience (and sometimes also the speaker—accounts vary), then it is not said/explicated. And this may be why these notions are ill-suited to the lying–misleading distinction. After all, one of the great things about a carefully truthful misleading is how seamlessly and automatically it takes place. The audience may well not explicitly represent to itself the proposition that the speaker *said*. It is often only much later, upon reflection (if at all), that one realizes what the speaker really *said*, in the sense relevant to the lying–misleading distinction. Consider, for example, Clinton's utterance of (1).

(1)   There is no improper relationship.

Clinton's deceptive ruse would be totally undermined if the audience consciously represented to themself as what is said the present-tense proposition that there is no improper relationship, only afterward inferring to a more sweeping denial. As soon as the audience realizes Clinton has only denied the relationship in the present tense, the attempt to mislead has failed. The misleading only succeeded as long as the audience *didn't* consciously represent this proposition as what Clinton said. Yet, even before the audience did this, it was in fact what Clinton said. To make sense of carefully constructed misleadings like this one, we need to allow for propositions that are said but *not* consciously represented by the audience.

1.2.2 Bach's impliciture For Bach, conversational implicitures must be meant. They are claims that the speaker means but does not explicitly say. But the notion of saying that we need for the lying–misleading distinction cannot be one that requires *being meant*, at least as that is standardly understood. On the usual understanding, if a speaker means something, she must intend (or at least expect) to convey it to her audience. A speaker cannot mean something and both expect and intend that her audience will never figure it out. And Bach certainly requires this.[1] In a great many cases, the careful, clever misleader does *not* mean what they say: they do not intend the audience to arrive at what is said as part of their interpretation. Rather, they intend the audience to be misled into believing something other than what was *said*, preferably without stopping to consider what is said. And if they are confident of their skill, they expect this. So the notion we need cannot be a part of speaker meaning.

1.2.3 Stanley's semantic content / what is said Stanley holds that "all the constituents of the propositions hearers would intuitively believe to be expressed by utterances are the result of assigning values to the elements of the sentence uttered, and combining them in accord with its structure" (2002: 149), and that they are therefore a part of semantic content. Reflection on what audiences understand is a key part of Stanley's method for discovering what is said. Once more, we can quickly see what poses problems for the lying–misleading distinction: the skilful misleader manages *not* to have the audience realize what she says. (At the point when Clinton's misleading was successful, the audience did not believe him to have made a present-tense denial of an improper relationship; they believed him to have tenselessly denied the relationship.)

Constrained conceptions of saying, then, fail to capture the lying–misleading distinction due to their focus on what speakers mean and what audiences understand. Considering the case of the skilful misleader makes it clear that this is not what is needed for this distinction.

---

[1] See e.g. Bach (1994: 125–6).

1.3 Austere conceptions

Austere conceptions move away from this psychological focus in a way that at first seems promising for the lying–misleading distinction. They do not require that what is said be meant or consciously represented by anyone, thus avoiding the problems that Constrained conceptions face from clever cases of misleading. Austere theories insist on extremely minimal contextual involvement in what is said, and most deny any role for speaker intentions in determining what is said. But it turns out that a theory which does not allow *any* role for speaker intentions in determining what is said simply cannot give plausible verdicts about what is said in many of the cases we have considered.

The most obvious problem case we have seen was that of demonstratives. On Bach's understanding of what is said, nothing truth evaluable is said when a sentence containing a demonstrative is uttered. If we used this understanding to draw the lying–misleading distinction, it clearly gives the wrong results. This has drastically counterintuitive consequences for our abilities both to lie and to speak the truth. Bach's what is said cannot be what we need for the lying–misleading distinction.

Borg agrees with Bach in ruling out speaker intentions as determinants of semantic content, but insists that semantic content can still contain referents for demonstratives. How this is meant to work is actually rather mysterious, but it does improve on Bach when it comes to capturing the lying–misleading distinction. Nonetheless, Borg's view still faces problems from Completion cases (like that of Fred, the murderous nurse).

Cappelen and Lepore are *not* opposed to giving a role to speaker intentions, and this allows them a non-mysterious way of getting referents for demonstratives. But they are still quite restrictive when it comes to contextual variation in semantic content, and as we have seen this means that their conception of semantic content cannot fulfil the role of saying for the lying–misleading distinction.

1.4 Lessened austerity: the importance of distinguishing between Completion and Expansion

Constrained and Unconstrained accounts both allowed far too much contextual involvement in what is said. But Austere accounts allowed too little. What we need, we saw in Chapter 2, is this a mostly Austere conception of saying, but one that allows demonstratives to contribute their referents to what is said and allows contextual supplementation in at least some Completion cases.

What is very striking about the notion of saying that we need for the lying–misleading distinction is that it seems that it should be one that rejects Expansion but accepts Completion. The reason we were able to reject all the Constrained accounts was that they all allowed Expansion. The examples of Billy at the Empire State Building, and of my careful misleading of Amanda's uncle, make it very clear that the notion of saying we need for the lying–misleading distinction will not be one that allows this. Yet later examples make it clear that we do need to allow Completion.

It took me quite a long time to notice this sharp intuitive difference between Expansion and Completion cases, because they are generally treated together. Theorists who accept one tend to accept the other. This is, I think, because Constrained theorists have quite a psychological focus, as we noted above—they are interested in what speakers mean, what audiences understand, or what is communicated. And it certainly is true that both Completion and Expansion (as I've defined them) are involved in all of these. And if we call any of these by the name 'what is said' (and all of them have been called this at one time or another), both Completion and Expansion will be involved in determining what is said. What's more, both will offer interesting examples of contextually supplied elements that are not called for by any obvious elements of the sentence uttered. But once we turn our attention to the notion of saying that we need for the lying–misleading distinction, things change.

So how can we capture this sort of notion of saying? As it turns out, there is more than one way to do this. (There may well even be others beyond those I sketch here.) In broadest outline, what I will do is to offer necessary conditions for a putative contextual contribution to be a part of what is said. My method will be to start from what a Constrained account would posit as what is said by a particular utterance of a sentence, and then to rule out those contextual contributions that should not be a part of what is said if we want to capture the lying–misleading distinction. By doing this, we will arrive at some constraints on an adequate understanding of what is said, for the purpose of the lying–misleading distinction.

2 Allowable contextual contributions

2.1 Only what's needed for truth evaluability

The obvious way to allow Completion and not Expansion is to only allow contextual supplementation that is needed in order to arrive at something truth evaluable as what is said. This gives us a necessary condition for some putative contextual contribution to make it into what is said by an utterance U of a sentence S.

A putative contextual contribution to what is said is a part of what is said only if without this contextually supplied material, utterance U of S would not say something truth evaluable.

But this criterion is ill-formulated for the job at hand. It uses the notion of saying as a part of a criterion to determine what is said. In order to know whether some putative element of what is said is *in fact* a part of what is said, we have to know what the utterance would say without it. But how are we to know that? Well, we have to test each putative contextual contribution against the criterion above . . . So this criterion leaves us with a highly problematic circularity.

To avoid this, we must use a different notion in our criterion. Interestingly, for all the disagreement in the debates on these matters, there is a quite startling degree of agreement over how to define 'semantic content', a notion which will serve quite nicely: Kent Bach, Robin Carston, Jeff King, and Jason Stanley are surprisingly similar in the way that they define 'semantic content'. This is startling because these theorists have very different views on what is actually included within semantic content—Stanley and King think it includes a huge range of contextual contributions, including those from what we have called Expansion and Completion. Bach and Carston think it is so minimal, and contains so few contextual contributions, that it rarely (if ever) amounts to a truth-evaluable proposition. But their actual definitions of semantic content are not so dramatically different from one another. Here are two, by way of illustration.

The semantic content of a sentence S in a context C is "the result of combining the referential contents of [an expression's] constituent terms relative to the context c in accord with the semantic composition rules corresponding to the syntactic structure of that expression". (King and Stanley 2005: 116)

The semantic content of a sentence S in a context C is what is said in that context, which is "determined compositionally by the semantic contents of the constituents ('elements') of the sentence as a function of their syntactic relationship . . . relative to [the] context". (Bach 2002: 22)

These definitions are really much the same. The vast differences between these accounts derive from differences regarding precisely what the constituents of a sentence are.

We can, then, draw on this agreement and rewrite our criterion as below, calling it 'NTE' (Needed for Truth Evaluability).

(NTE)A putative contextual contribution to what is said is a part of what is said only if without this contextually supplied material, S would not have a truth-evaluable semantic content in C.[2]

This is an improvement. It is not circular. And it rules out Expansion cases, since those are ones in which contextually supplied material is added which is not necessary in order to arrive at a truth-evaluable semantic content. It allows for contextually supplied references for demonstratives, since these are needed in order to arrive at truth-evaluable semantic content. And it allows Completion cases, since it does not rule out contextual material in what is said which is needed to arrive at a truth-evaluable semantic content.

But we do not yet have a clear answer about what happens for particular examples of Completion we have seen. What we do not yet know is whether any contextually supplied material other than the referents of obvious indexical terms will pass the criterion (NTE). To see this problem, consider that on Emma Borg's view or Cappelen and Lepore's, (2) has a perfectly truth-evaluable semantic content without any contextual supplementation.

(2)   Dave's had enough.

For Borg, (2) has as its semantic content the perfectly truth-evaluable proposition that Fred has had enough of something. For Cappelen and Lepore it has as its semantic content the perfectly truth-evaluable proposition that Fred has had enough. On either of their views, then, (NTE) rules

---

[2] Note that I need not take a view on whether these contributions make it into semantic content. Bach and Carston would say that they do not, while King and Stanley would say that they do.

out completing what is said by an utterance of (2) with a specification of what Dave has had enough of.

In order to avoid these results, we need to take a view on the semantic contents of various sorts of terms. Again, interestingly, Bach's, Stanley's, and Carston's would all be perfectly fine. For on all of these views—no matter how much they differ in other ways—sentences containing terms such as 'enough' do not express a truth-evaluable semantic content without contextual supplementation. We must, however, reject Borg's view on these terms. Once more, we will follow this consensus. As a result, (NTE) will allow contextual contributions to what is said in these cases.

2.2 Selecting contextual contributions

2.2.1 Cases of conflict   One issue that has been surprisingly neglected in discussions of Completion is that of how it is that contextually supplied material is determined. Theorists will slide back and forth between discussing the audience's interpretation, the speaker's intention, and what is salient, seemingly without realizing this. The reason for this is that their focus has been on cases where all of these converge—these are, after all, the cases in which the case for such contextual contributions is strongest. But attention to the issues we are considering here quickly pushes us to consider the cases where these diverge. (Consider, for example, the variants of the Empire State Building example, which made crucial use of such divergences to show the problematic nature of Expansion.)

As I've noted, the clearest cases will be ones where the speaker intends the completion, the completion is salient, and the audience grasps it. Take, for example, the case of Fred, the murderous nurse who wants to kill his patient Dave by denying him heart medication. Ed holds up the bottle of heart medicine, with a questioning look, and Fred responds with (2).

(2)   Dave's had enough.

Fred means *Dave's had enough heart medicine*; Ed takes Fred to mean *Dave's had enough heart medicine*; and *heart medicine* is clearly salient. This is a clear case of lying, and it seems also to be a clear case of Completion—with *heart medicine*.[3] One thought worth trying out is that all of these are necessary

---

[3] Actually, we will shortly be raising worries about exactly what the correct Completion is.

conditions for a completion to make it into what is said: the completion must be meant by the speaker, grasped by the audience, and salient.

We can quickly see, however, that this is asking too much. Imagine now that the scenario is just like that described above, with the same questioning look and the same reply—but that Ed mishears Fred's reply, and thinks that he has uttered (4), which he takes to be an indirect way of indicating that Dave needs more medicine:

(4) Dave's looking rough.

In this case, fortuitously for Dave, Ed does not grasp Fred's intended completion. But we have no doubt that Fred has nonetheless lied. The false claim that Fred is trying to convey is that *Dave's had enough heart medicine*. Call this P. In order for Fred to lie with his utterance, the first necessary condition is that he must have said that P. The fact that we have no doubt that Fred has lied shows that we take *Dave's had enough heart medicine* to be said, even though the audience fails to grasp *heart medicine* as a completion (and indeed fails to grasp most of the utterance). Audience uptake, then, cannot be a necessary condition for a contextually supplied completion to be a part of what is said.

Now we're left with salience and speaker intention to consider as possible necessary conditions. It is much trickier to be sure about these, it seems to me. First, take salience. What we need to consider is a possible completion that is not salient. Imagine, for example, that Ed has been making pleasant conversation with Dave about the weather, and is getting up to bring him a cup of tea. Murderous Fred walks in, and falsely takes Ed to be about to give Dave his much-needed heart medication. Thinking to prevent this, he utters (2):

(2) Dave's had enough.

Fred's intended completion for (1) is *heart medicine*, but *heart medicine* is not at all salient, and in fact Ed takes Fred to be warning him against giving Fred another cup of tea. Now we must ask ourselves, has Fred lied? In order for Fred to have lied, he must have said that Dave's had enough heart medicine. I think intuitions here are extremely unclear. For now, we'll just note this point: we're not quite sure whether salience is a necessary condition for a putative completion to make it into what is said.

Things are similarly unclear with respect to speaker intention as a necessary condition, but for slightly different reasons. Imagine now a slightly different scene. Gertrude, a not-at-all-murderous but somewhat near-sighted nurse, is in the room with Ed and Dave. Ed holds up the heart medicine and looks at Gertrude quizzically. Gertrude, unable to see what Ed is holding up, takes him to be holding up a whisky bottle. She correctly takes Dave to have had enough whisky, and therefore utters (2):

(2)   Dave's had enough.

Gertrude's intended completion is *whisky*. But what is salient, and what the audience takes to be her intended completion, is *heart medicine*. So what do our intuitions say about this example? It seems to me that they are quite unclear about what she has said. Has she *said* that Dave's had enough heart medicine? If so, then she accidentally said something false. But it seems equally reasonable to suggest that she said that Dave's had enough whisky, which is true. Or that she failed to say anything truth evaluable, due to the confusion. No matter what, it's clear that she didn't lie. But there are a number of different ways to get this result. Recall our definition of 'Lying':

> Lying:If the speaker is not the victim of linguistic error/malapropism or using metaphor, hyperbole, or irony, then they lie iff (1) they say that P; (2) they believe P to be false;[4] (3) they take themself to be in a warranting context.

Take P to be *Dave's had enough heart medicine*. (This is the false claim that Gertrude *might* have said.) If Gertrude failed to say anything, or if she said that Dave's had enough whisky, then she hasn't lied because she hasn't said that P. If she did say it, however, it seems perfectly reasonable to cast her confusion as a sort of linguistic error and deny that she has lied on these grounds.[5] But has she accidentally said something false? Again, I think intuitions are very unclear. It seems to me equally acceptable to maintain that Gertrude said nothing, that she accidentally said a falsehood about heart medicine, or that she said something true about whisky. Again, we'll come back to this unclarity.

What do we know now? We know that a Completion may be a part of what is said even if it is not understood by the audience. But we're not sure whether it needs to be salient to the audience. Nor are we sure whether it

---

[4] Those who think that lies must be false would rephrase this as "they truly believe P to be false".

[5] One with qualms about this move could add on an additional clause relating to confusion about referents of demonstratives, but this seems to me unnecessary.

needs to be intended by the speaker. Reflecting on judgements about lying and misleading fails to give us clear guidance on these questions. I think there is good reason for this. In order to make use of the lying–misleading distinction, it is not necessary to have a conception of saying with clear verdicts in every case. Think, for example, of the case we've just looked at, in which the heart medicine is the salient completion, although not intended by Gertrude, the speaker. The question we're trying to answer is whether she unintentionally said something about the heart medicine. But we're just not sure. We *know* that she didn't lie, even without a verdict on exactly what she said. And that's all we need for the lying–misleading distinction. We lack a verdict on whether she accidentally said something false, but that's really not very important to us in drawing the (apparently) moral distinction between lying and misleading. One way or another, she didn't lie. The previous case, in which Dave utters (1) with the intention of saying something about heart medicine, but the heart medicine fails to be salient, is slightly different. Whether or not Dave says something about heart medicine determines whether or not Dave lied.

For now, we'll rest content with the necessary condition (NTE) for being said, combined with a view like Bach's, Stanley's, or Carston's on both the nature of semantic content and the semantic contents of terms like 'enough'.

(NTE)A putative contextual contribution to what is said is a part of what is said only if without this contextually supplied material, S would not have a truth-evaluable semantic content in C.

But we should bear in mind that when speaker intentions, audience interpretations, and salience are in tension with each other, there will be a range of unclear cases.

2.2.2 Cases of unclarity In the last section, we looked at cases in which disagreements between speaker intentions, audience interpretations, and salience gave rise to murky (or non-existent) intuitions. But even when we don't have such disagreements, what is said may be—in a different way—unclear.

To see this, let's return to a much clearer version of the case of Fred the murderous nurse, one in which there is no misunderstanding or disagreement about what is said.

Dave is lying in bed, and two nurses are discussing the treatment he needs. Ed holds up a bottle of heart medicine, points at it, and utters (5):

(5)   Has Dave had enough?

Fred replies with (2):

(2)   Dave's had enough.

As it turns out, Fred hates Dave, wants him to die, and plans to bring this about by denying him his much-needed heart medicine. When he uttered (2), Fred meant something like (2*), which he knew to be false.

(2*)   Dave's had enough heart medicine.

Intuitively, Fred has lied. We need to capture this intuition.

It is clear that the completion in (2*) meets (NTE). As we've already seen, without contextual supplementation the semantic content of (2) is not a truth-evaluable proposition. But the problem is that other completions might also work, and work just as well. (2**) and (2***), among others, are also possible completions:

(2**)   Dave's had enough of that.
(2***)   Dave's had enough of the stuff in that bottle you're holding up.

All of these, intuitively are perfectly natural candidates for what is said. Any of them would give the verdict that Fred is lying. It is difficult to imagine that anything about Ed's interpretation of Dave's intentions would fix one of these rather than another as what is said. Clearly, what's said by (2) involves some sort of Completion—but it is very hard to see how we can get an answer as to what exactly that Completion is.

2.2.2.1 OPTION 1: *DE RE* COMPLETIONS

This sort of issue does not receive much attention in most discussions. The assumption seems to be that speaker intentions, salience, or audience interpretation will suffice to pick out a particular one of these completions. Rey Elugardo and Rob Stainton, however, have argued very plausibly (2004: 459) that such intentions or interpretations are not sufficient to select one rather than another of these completions. This allows them, we saw in Chapter 2, to argue against Jason Stanley's suggestion that many apparent Completion cases are really cases of syntactic ellipsis. They point out that syntactic ellipsis would require one rather than another of the linguistic alternatives to be actually present somehow in the sentence uttered, and maintain that these is no way to select one of these as the one that's present.

Stainton's (2006) solution to this difficulty is to claim that *de re completions* take place: that is, the speaker's intentions determine a certain object as a propositional constituent, and this object completes the proposition, making it truth evaluable. So in the case of Fred the murderous nurse, the bottle of medicine *itself* (rather than any particular way of referring to it) is a part of what is said by Fred's utterance of (2). This way, there is no need to select between propositions like (2), (2*), and (2**).

Stainton's view on Completion would easily allow us to accommodate the intuition that Fred has lied: it give us a proposition that was said, and this was the stumbling block for accommodating the claim that Fred has lied. But the view is not so appealing for all cases.

Consider now a scenario in which I know that Helga is ready for many things: she's ready to leave the house, she's ready to go to the party, and she's ready to see Iggy, who will take her to the party. I, however, am trying to sabotage Helga's budding friendship with Iggy, a known despiser of the unpunctual. Iggy shows up at the house and asks for Helga. I utter (6), without any thought of whether I mean (6*), (6**), or (6***).

(6)   Sorry, Iggy—Helga's not ready.
(6*)   Sorry, Iggy—Helga's not ready to leave the house.
(6**)   Sorry, Iggy—Helga's not ready for the party.
(6***) Sorry, Iggy—Helga's not ready to see you.

Iggy goes off in a huff, resolving never to make plans with Helga again, and my evil intentions are fulfilled. Intuitively, I have lied. It would not be at all convincing for me to maintain either that I said something true—because there is of course something that Helga's not ready for (perhaps the US presidency); or that I have failed to say anything because I didn't specify what Helga was ready for. We want, then, to find a way to say that I have lied. This requires some proposition that I have said, but it is very hard to say what de re completion could reasonably be claimed as that proposition. This is not a case in which there is one object, describable in different ways. Instead, my intended meaning seems to be indeterminate across a range of possible completions given by (6*)–(6***), which cannot be understood as ways of describing a single object.

2.2.2.2 OPTION 2: INDETERMINATE COMPLETION

This suggests a different sort of solution. Instead, one might claim that the completion of (6) is indeterminate across a range of possible completions, where these are restricted by speaker intentions, audience interpretation, and salience. (When these agree, things are fairly simple; we've seen that when they don't agree intuitions are very murky.) It's clear, for example, that (6) is not to be completed by *the US presidency*; and that (6*)–(6***) would be perfectly acceptable completions. None of these completions on its own, then, has any claim to be the right one, although the range of acceptable completions does have a claim to correctness. Call this the Indeterminate Completion view.

As yet, it is poorly specified. Is the idea that what is said in these cases is an indeterminate proposition? Or is the thought that what is said is somehow indeterminate across a range of precise propositions? These questions will be familiar from discussions of supervaluationism. They are serious and difficult ones, and it is genuinely unclear how to settle them. I hope to largely avoid them here, as they don't seem to make a difference to the lying–misleading distinction. For simplicity, I'll assume that what is said is indeterminate across a range of precise propositions.

We can make sense of the idea of saying something false with an utterance of (6) by drawing upon insights from supervaluationism to claim that I have said something false—because what I have said is false on every acceptable completion. But it is a bit trickier to make sense of the thought that I have lied. Our definition of 'lying' is couched in terms of a single proposition that is said:

> Lying: If the speaker is not the victim of linguistic error/malapropism or using metaphor, hyperbole, or irony, then they lie iff (1) they say that P; (2) they believe P to be false;[6] (3) they take themself to be in a warranting context.

This needs modification if we are to adopt the Indeterminate Completion view. In order to satisfy this definition, there has to be some particular proposition that is said, believed/known by the speaker to be false, and which the speaker intends her audience to believe. When what is said is

---

[6] Those who think that lies must be false would rephrase this as "they truly believe P to be false".

indeterminate, there does not seem to be such a proposition. We can, however, make some slight alterations to deal with this.

We'll call the full definition Lying (Complete). It includes two conditions, (A) and (B), but (A) is really just a special case of (B).

Lying (Complete):

If the speaker is not the victim of linguistic error/malapropism or using metaphor, hyperbole, or irony, then they lie iff (A) or (B) holds:

(A) (1) They say that P; (2) They believe P to be false; (3) They take themself to be in a warranting context.[7]

(B) (1) They say something indeterminate across a range of acceptable complete propositions, CP1 ... CPn); (2) for each complete proposition in the range CP1 ... CPn, they believe that proposition to be false; (3) They take themself to be in a warranting context.[8]

Now we have a definition with the (desired) consequence that I have lied. For each of the completed propositions (e.g. (6*), (6**), (6***)...), I know that proposition is false and I intend my audience to believe that it is true. One might worry that I am not consciously representing each of these propositions to myself, and so couldn't be said to intend my audience to believe each of them. This, however, is the familiar problem of tacit psychological states. Any plausible theory of intentions has to allow for intentions that are not consciously, explicitly represented by the agent, so this is not particularly a problem for this view.

The Indeterminate Completion view gives us an alternative to the *de re completion* view. Moreover, it is one with more plausibility for examples like my malicious utterance of (6). However, it needs a great deal more work. In particular, there are difficult issues about how the range of possible completions is to be determined, and about how precise this range is. Fully developing a view of saying which includes the Indeterminate Completion view would be a formidable task, which would take us too far afield. I will mostly suppress these complications for the remainder of the book.

---

[7] One who believes that lies must be false would add that P must be false.
[8] One who believes that lies must be false would add that CP1 ... CPn must be false.

3 Conclusion

What I have offered in this chapter is a sketch of the sort of conception of what is said that we need for the lying–misleading distinction. (This sketch can be understood as something like a constraint on a satisfactory conception of saying for the lying–misleading distinction.) This conception of what is said allows contextual contributions to what is said only if (NTE) holds for that putative contextual contribution, and only if we reject an understanding like Borg's of terms like 'enough'. Our procedure is to begin with what a Constrained conception of what is said would countenance, and then to test each putative contextual contribution against (NTE).

> (NTE) A putative contextual contribution to what is said is a part of what is said only if without this contextually supplied material, S would not have a truth-evaluable semantic content in C.

It is less austere than the Austere views we examined in Chapter 2, and more austere than the Constrained and Unconstrained views. One key feature of this sort of view is that it judges Completion to be acceptable and Expansion to be unacceptable—unlike other available views. I showed that I could get this result—and also allow demonstrative references into what is said—by testing putative contextual contributions to what is said against the criterion I called (NTE), which allows such contributions only if their absence from semantic content would result in a semantic content that is not truth evaluable. However, some uncertainties remain.

(1) Once (NTE) has told us which utterances are eligible for Completion, it is still not entirely clear which completions make it into what is said, and which do not: must they be salient? Must they be intended by the speaker?

(2) It is far from clear how we should treat cases in which a completion is, broadly speaking, quite obvious to all—but in which the precise nature of the completion is underspecified. There are at least two possible approaches, Stainton's de re approach and what I have called the Indeterminate Completion view. Both of these views would require considerably more work to be fully defensible.

I have suggested that uncertainty (1) is likely to remain—and should remain—an uncertainty. We do not need to settle it in order to draw the lying–misleading distinction—at least with respect to our moral concerns. (I'll elaborate on this in Chapter 4.) Uncertainty (2) is different. It is not a matter of unclear intuitions about which cases are cases of lying or misleading; or even of unclear intuitions about what is said. Instead, the problem is one of finding the right technical way to capture the intuitions that we have. This is something I'm postponing for another time, as pursuing it would take me away from my primary interest in the lying–misleading distinction. Instead, I want to reflect briefly on the relationship between the view of saying developed here and Grice's own views.

In Chapter 2, we began our discussion of what is said with Grice—the traditional starting point for such discussions. A case might be made that Grice would in fact be quite sympathetic to where we have ended up. Here were the key points I drew out about Grice's own conception of what is said:

1. What is said is very closely linked to the sentence uttered, and varies very little from one context to another (unlike what is conversationally implicated).
2. What is said by a sentence containing an ambiguous word such as 'bank' can vary from one context to another.
3. Truth value is determined by what is said. Moreover, if something is not relevant to truth value, it is not a part of what is said, even if it is a part of the meaning of the sentence uttered.

Grice did not consider cases of Completion, or cases of contextual variation other than ambiguity. If we let these things into what is said, then what is said is less closely linked to the sentence uttered than Grice seemed to allow. If we don't let them into what is said, though, we end up without truth values for what is said in a huge number of cases (arguably, most utterances will be like this). And this seems to go against Grice's view that truth value is determined by what is said. As we have seen, there are a number of ways one could deal with this situation.

The lying–misleading distinction, we have seen, requires us to find a conception of what is said that allows contextual contributions when they are needed to arrive at something truth evaluable (NTE). This seems to me to be a good fit with much of what Grice did say about what is said. In particular, it fits well with his use of what is said as the bearer of truth value, and with his desire to avoid contextual contributions beyond those that really are necessary for it to serve this purpose.

It must be admitted, however, that this does not fit with everything that Grice said about what is said. In particular, it fits badly with Grice's frequently neglected commitment to the idea that anything which is said must be meant.[9] But this commitment (a notably unpopular one among subsequent thinkers) is clearly one that must be abandoned if we are to capture the notion that we need for the lying–misleading distinction. As we have noted, in the cleverest cases of mere misleading the speaker does not *mean* the true proposition that is said, since their plan is that the audience will not grasp and reflect on it, instead leaping straight to a false proposition.

The conception of what is said that we've arrived at, then, is not strictly Grice's. No conception that gives any verdict at all about Completion cases and contextual variation (other than that involved in ambiguity) is strictly Gricean. Nor is any conception that fails to require that speakers mean what is said. It is, however, Gricean in the importance it places on having a truth-evaluable proposition as what is said, and in making sure that the contextual variation allowed is no more than is needed for this. Moreover, it's very Gricean in its insistence that what is said must be something on which speakers have some sort of intuitive grip. (This can be contrasted with, e.g. Emma Borg's semantic content, which she takes to be very much a theoretician's notion.) Indeed, this is built into the very starting point for the book: the desire to arrive at a notion of that can work for the very intuitive and ordinary lying–misleading distinction.

---

[9]   This commitment is made explicit in Grice (1989: 87).

4

Is Lying Worse than Merely Misleading?[1]

Alasdair MacIntyre (1994) has argued that there are two broad traditions when it comes to the morality of lying. One tradition defines lying quite broadly and permits lies with certain motivations, or lies with certain consequences. This tradition would tend to count any deliberate deception as a lie, but to insist that some of these lies are not morally problematic. The other tradition claims that lies are never permissible, but it defines lying very strictly, so that many deceptions are not lies.[2] It is much easier to justify the first tradition's view—after all, this tradition judges a deception by its motivations or its consequences—and there is nothing surprising about the claim that these are of moral relevance. The second tradition's view is much more puzzling: according to this tradition, one act of deception could be better than another, despite having the very same consequences and motivation. It could be morally superior simply due to the *method* of deception chosen.[3]

The lying–misleading distinction is completely irrelevant to the first tradition, as for that tradition what matters is consequences and motivations.

---

[1] There is a large literature in ethics on deception and related issues. However, most of this literature does not specifically address the distinction between lying and merely misleading, which is my focus here. Here I am focusing only on attempts to justify a moral preference for merely misleading over lying, rather than beginning with accounts of what is wrong with lying or deception.

[2] For a nice discussion of the careful way that Kant limits what counts as a lie, see Mahon (2003).

[3] It is important to be careful about but what exactly is puzzling here. The puzzle doesn't arise from the acts of lying and misleading being precisely the same sort of acts. They're not: they're different acts, because they're acts of deceiving in different ways. The puzzle is why these difference should be taken to be morally significant. Or, more precisely, why acts of deceiving via one method should seem morally superior to acts of deceiving via a different method. (For more on this point, see Adler (2010).)

(Adherents to this tradition are likely to see followers of the second tradition as "fetishizing assertion", to use Bernard Williams's nice phrase.)[4] For the second tradition, however, the lying–misleading distinction is of vital significance. According to this tradition, acts of deception that are mere misleadings are morally better than acts of deception that are lies. This means that acts of deception that are lies are (holding all else fixed) worse than acts of deception which are mere misleadings. This tradition has had many proponents, and many people seem to find it quite instinctively appealing.

St Athanasius, mentioned earlier, clearly adhered to this view. This is why he thought it so important to tell his pursuers, "Athanasius is not far from here" rather than saying something clearly false such as, "Athanasius is miles away!".

Belief that lying is worse than misleading is (at least sometimes) what motivates an unfaithful partner to answer "I've been working late a lot" rather than "no", when asked, "are you having an affair?". This is really a very puzzling thing: surely he cannot really think that his partner will feel better about a discovered infidelity if she also realizes that he never *said* anything false. In this sort of situation, the pain caused is in no way mitigated by misleading rather than lying. Why, then, take the trouble to do it?

Importantly, however, many of us do take this sort of trouble. It feels perhaps most legitimate in cases of deception for the sake of kindness. Let's return to an example I introduced in the preface. An elderly woman is dying. She asks if her son is well. You saw him yesterday (at which point he was happy and healthy), but you know that shortly after your meeting he was hit by a truck and killed. Many people would, I think, have the intuition that it is better to utter (1) than (2)—because (1) is merely misleading while (2) is a lie.

(1)   I saw him yesterday and he was happy and healthy.
(2)   He's happy and healthy.

This preference really is very strange: if we think it is right to protect the elderly woman from knowing the truth, why does it matter whether we do this by lying or misleading? If we think it's wrong, why is that wrong mitigated if we do it via misleading?

The first thing I will do in this chapter is to show, by way of counterexamples, that it is simply false to claim that misleading is always preferable to lying. But it would be wrong to move from this to a total dismissal of

---

[4] Williams (2002: 100).

the second tradition. For there is another alternative available: this is to maintain that proponents of the second tradition have overstated their claim. They should not have been defending a universal preference for misleading over lying, but only a defeasible one. This is, indeed, a possible view. I will argue, however, that it is far more appealing to offer an alternative explanation for the intuitions that have seemed to favour the second tradition. This explanation takes very seriously the moral motivation for misleading rather than lying, while at the same time denying that acts of misleading are in general morally preferable to acts of lying. In so doing, it represents an alternative that is distinct from, yet draws on, both traditions. It rejects the claim that misleading is better than lying, while at the same time recognizing and making sense of the significance of this distinction to moral psychology.

1 Clarifications

Before we begin in earnest, though, a few clarifications are in order. Clarification is needed because of the following complications:

- 'Misleading', unlike 'lying', is a success term.[5] A has not misled B unless B believes A. A can, however, lie to B even if B does not believe A. In order to pinpoint the issue correctly, successful lying is what should be compared to misleading; and lying should be compared to attempting to mislead.
- Lying, unlike misleading, must be deliberate. I cannot accidentally lie to you, but I can accidentally mislead you. There is absolutely no puzzle about why lying should be morally worse than accidental misleading—deliberately doing something bad is uncontroversially morally worse than accidentally doing something bad. My focus, then, is on the puzzling cases: those in which we contrast lying with deliberate misleading.
- It is not hard to see why it is worse to lie to my partner about whether I'm having an affair than to mislead someone about how much I like to eat peas. The puzzle that is our focus here is why it is that lying should be worse than misleading, *when we hold everything else fixed.*

---

[5] 'Success term' is perhaps not quite the right phrase, given that misleading can, as noted above, be unintentional.

For convenience, let's call the precise version of the claim that misleading is morally preferable to lying '(M)':

> (M)   Holding all else fixed, lying is morally worse than merely deliberately attempting to mislead; and successful lying is morally worse than merely deliberately misleading.

I will sometimes write more loosely, referring to the question of whether lying is morally worse than misleading. But claim (M) is really what I am interested in.

2 Counter-examples

In this section, I offer what seem to me to be compelling cases in which there does not seem to be a moral reason for preferring misleading to lying. That is, I offer counter-examples to (M).

> (M)   Holding all else fixed, lying is morally worse than merely deliberately attempting to mislead; and successful lying is morally worse than merely deliberately misleading.

2.1 Charla, Dave, and HIV

Charla is HIV positive, but she does not yet have AIDS, and she knows both of these facts. Dave is about to have sex with Charla for the first time, and, cautiously but imprecisely, he asks (3).

> (3)   Do you have AIDS?

Charla replies with (4).

> (4)   No, I don't have AIDS.

Charla and Dave have unprotected sex, and Dave becomes infected with HIV. It is unquestionably true that Charla deceived Dave about her HIV status, and also unquestionably true that Charla did not lie—she merely misled him. Yet it seems completely absurd to suppose that Charla's deception was even a tiny bit better due to her avoidance of lying. In this case, misleading is in no way morally preferable to lying. If misleading was, quite generally, morally preferable to lying, it would be morally preferable in this case. Since it is not, we should reject the strong general claim (M).

2.2 George and the peanut oil

George makes dinner for Frieda. He knows that Frieda has a peanut allergy so virulent that even a small amount of peanut oil could kill her. He wants to kill Frieda, so he has cooked with peanut oil. Frieda, being rightly cautious, asks whether George has put any peanuts in the meal. George utters the true but misleading (5) rather than the false (6).

(5) No, I didn't put any peanuts in.
(6) No, it's perfectly safe for you to eat.

Again, it does not seem likely to me that anyone would think this choice of George's makes his act even slightly better.

2.3 The murderer at the door

Further evidence against (M) perhaps comes from cases where neither lying nor misleading seems problematic—though I am less certain about this. Take, for example, the classic case of the murderer at the door asking about the location of his intended victim (and making it clear that murder is indeed his goal). Kant infamously thought that even in this case lying would be wrong, and that one should try to mislead. Most of us, however, react differently. We think that one should do whatever is most likely to succeed in the goal of preventing murder—and that there is absolutely no moral difficulty with lying to the murderer. Moreover, we don't think it's somehow worse to do this by lying rather than misleading.[6] If we really, on reflection, believed (M), we would not have this reaction.[7]

3 A defeasible claim?

Even if we accept the above counter-examples to (M)[8] we need not wholly reject the second tradition. One could argue, instead, that the theorists of the second tradition have overstated their claim. They should

---

[6] Indeed, we think there is something wrong with a person who worried about formulating his utterance in just the right way to avoid lying.

[7] Obviously, there are some people—like Kant—who disagree. But they are very much in a minority. Some such people will probably not be moved by any of the counter-examples to (M) suggested in this section. But they will still need to face the challenges of justification raised in the next section.

[8] Which we needn't: we could insist that there are slight differences in wrongdoing depending on which utterance is chosen but that the gravity of the wrong (or the importance

instead have argued for a defeasible moral preference for misleading over lying—one that generally holds but in certain very special cases does not. Perhaps instead they should have argued for what I call (M-D):

> (M-D)   Except in certain special cases: holding all else fixed, lying is morally worse than merely deliberately attempting to mislead; and successful lying is morally worse than merely deliberately misleading.

This claim would be unaffected by the counter-examples I have offered, if one could plausibly argue that they are the sorts of special cases at issue. Instead, these counter-examples would be treated as special cases, and perhaps a story could even be told about why these cases are special. Ordinary intuitions would, I am sure, be better captured by (M-D) than by (M). And perhaps some (though clearly not all) supporters of (M) would happily switch allegiance to (M-D) once they have reflected on the counter-examples to (M).

So now we have a claim, (M-D), which is immune to our earlier counter-examples.[9] But counter-examples are not the only problems faced by defenders of the second tradition. The far larger problem is that of how to justify a moral distinction that seems so puzzling. What is required is some sort of explanation of why we shouldn't be puzzled after all by a moral preference (even a defeasible one) for misleading over lying.

3.1 Kant/MacIntyre: different duties

MacIntyre (1994: 337) interprets Kant as claiming that:

my duty is to assert [in our terms, say] only what is true and the mistaken inferences which others may draw from what I say or what I do are ... not my responsibility, but theirs.[10]

---

of the good action, in the case of the murderer at the door) that is done by either utterance makes this difficult for us to discern.

[9] A full defence of (M-D) would also require some effort to work out which sorts of special cases are exceptions and why this should be. But since I won't be defending (M-D), I won't worry about this here. Strudler (2010) offers a view of this sort, where he makes an exception for views on which the deception by misleading is maximally wrong, and so can't be made worse if accomplished by lying.

[10] Quite strangely, MacIntyre has the words "in some cases at least" where I have " ... ". This is strange, because he is discussing a justification for the wholly universal claim that lying is always wrong.

The idea here is that my duty is confined to the truth of what I assert. On this interpretation, the beliefs of others are simply no responsibility of mine, as long as I have asserted only true things.

At first, this view seems appealing. It's not completely unintuitive to suppose that my duties concern only what I do, and not what others do. Indeed, this seems quite reasonable. But the problem is that when I deliberately mislead, I attempt to induce a false belief in someone else. This is something that *I do*.[11] It is very difficult to see why I should not have a duty to refrain from doing this, if I have a duty to refrain from asserting (or saying) what is false. To merely state that my duties are confined to the truth of my assertions is not any justification at all. If I have a duty not to say false things to the dying woman, why don't I also have a duty not to deliberately mislead her? If Athanasius doesn't have a duty not to mislead his pursuers, why should he have a duty not to say false things to them? The crucial questions are simply not answered. We need to know *why* my duties are confined to avoiding falsehood in what I assert.

3.2 *Chisholm and Feehan: breach of faith*

Chisholm and Feehan argue that a liar violates the audience's trust in a way that a misleader does not. According to them, an audience has a *right to expect* that the speaker believes what is said to true, but no such right with respect to other claims that are conveyed. As a result, they claim, "lying, unlike other types of intended deception, is essentially a breach of faith" (1977: 153).[12] They support this claim by comparing lying with a case of non-linguistic deception—Kant's example of packing a bag in order to bring about a false belief that one is leaving on a trip.

It is more difficult, however, to support Chisholm and Feehan's claim when we turn our attention to linguistic examples, and particularly to Gricean conversational implicatures. Conversational implicatures are, roughly, claims that the audience needs to take the speaker to be trying to communicate in order to understand the speaker as cooperative. The speaker relies on the audience's assumption of cooperativeness in order to communicate these claims. So, for example, take the conversation below:

---

[11] Williams makes a point similar to this on 108.
[12] This idea (among others) is invoked by Green (2001: 160) in order to argue for the moral soundness of the distinctions drawn by US perjury law between lying and merely misleading.

A: "Does your office have a working heater?"
B: "I had to order electric gloves from Hong Kong last winter!"

If we look just at what's said, B's response seems completely uncooperative. A has asked a question about heaters, and B has responded by talking about gloves. But A probably won't see B's response as irrelevant in this way, because A will want to preserve the assumption that B is being cooperative. A can do this by assuming B is trying to communicate that her heater worked so poorly that she had to order electric gloves to stay warm. This claim, then, is conversationally implicated.[13] Conversational implicatures are often exploited as a way to mislead without lying.

One example of this is my utterance of the true (7) to Amanda's uncle:

(7)   Amanda and Beau got married and had children.

Amanda's uncle, as I intend him to, takes from this the message that Amanda and Beau's marriage preceded the childbirth. And this is precisely what one should expect. After all, he assumes that I am being cooperative. One of Grice's maxims of conversation is the maxim of manner, which dictates that one list events in the order in which they occurred. In order to understand me as cooperative, Amanda's uncle *must* assume that I am following the maxim of manner, so he is required to assume that I believed the marriage to precede the children. Can it really be true that, in spite of all this, he has *no right* to expect that I think the wedding preceded the children? This seems patently wrong. Chisholm and Feehan's view is plausible enough when we compare lies to non-linguistic deception. Arguably packing a bag does not give the audience a right to expect that one is leaving on a trip. But linguistic deception—and perhaps particularly linguistic deception by means of conversational implicature—is a different matter.[14]

Once more, we have the lying–misleading distinction explained in terms of another distinction: that between what the audience has a right to expect the speaker to believe and what the audience does not have a right to expect the speaker to believe. Chisholm and Feehan maintain that the audience only has a right to expect the speaker to believe what she *says*.

---

[13] There are actually lots of complexities about how conversational implicatures work which I am suppressing as they're irrelevant to the topic at hand. But for more on these, see Davis (1998, 2005, 2007); Saul (2001, 2002).

[14] Jonathan Adler (1997: 444) raises a similar objection.

But they give no convincing argument for this, and there's a good case to be made that the audience has a right to expect more than this.

3.3 Caveat Auditor

Related to, but distinct from, these explanations, is Stuart Green's claim that a principle of Caveat Auditor applies to misleadings but not to lies: "A listener is responsible for ascertaining that a statement is true before believing it" (2006: 165). The idea, presumably is that we are entitled to simply believe what is *said* to us (by an apparently sincere speaker, I assume), but if something is not said but merely communicated, we have no such entitlement. It is, once more, puzzling to see how and why this particular rule might come to be in force. But, more importantly, it is also surely wrong to think that it is in force. Imagine what it would mean if it was, by contrasting these two conversations.

Conversation 1
Amanda: Where does the visiting speaker want to go to dinner, the Thai restaurant or the Ethiopian?
Beau: She says she likes Ethiopian.

Conversation 2
Amanda: Where does the visiting speaker want to go to dinner, the Thai restaurant or the Ethiopian?
Beau: She wants to go to the Ethiopian.

In Conversation 2, Amanda gets a direct answer to her question, while in Conversation 1 this is merely implicated. If Green is right, the responsible audience should feel an obligation to ascertain that *she wants to go to the Ethiopian* is true in the first case, but not in the second. It may not take much to do this, since the implicature is a pretty clear one. But there is an additional obligation. It seems to me extremely unlikely that any audience will feel that there is this obligation, or even notice the difference between the cases. Moreover, cases like this arise all the time in normal conversation—again without even being noticed. It does not seem, then, that the norm Green suggests is actually in force.[15]

---

[15] This fits well with Bernard Williams's (2002: 100, 110) observation that in circumstances of "normal trust" we are entitled to (and do) rely on what people implicate just as much as on what they say.

3.4 Effort and sacrifice

In his (forthcoming), Jonathan Adler suggests that one key difference between lying and merely misleading is that merely misleading requires "more effort than lying without compensating assurance for generating the false belief" (10). This, he takes it, might demonstrate to the victim (if the deception becomes known) a greater respect both for the victim and for the truth.

I agree with Adler that careful misleading is likely to require a bit more work, and also that it won't compensate for this by increasing the chance of generating a false belief. However, I am not convinced that this can help to ground an ethical difference. One reason is that misleading does offer a different compensation for this small amount of extra work: it offers deniability ("I didn't mean to suggest *that!*"); and it also offers the likelihood of being let off the hook by those who take misleading to be ethically better than lying.

More importantly, though, we don't generally think that choosing more effortful wrongdoing with less chance of success makes one's wrongdoing any *better* ethically. Consider, for example, a right-handed football hooligan who decides to only punch people with his left hand—because this takes more effort, without a compensating increase in likelihood of seriously hurting his victim. Despite this bizarre choice, he works very hard to achieve the same result: major damage to his victim. Do we think this hooligan is better than one who goes ahead and uses his right hand? No, I don't think that we do. So I'm unconvinced that the greater effort and diminished likelihood of success make the act of misleading any better than the act of lying.

I do, however, think that Adler is getting at something right—*for some cases*—when he writes that "The misleading implicature is an effortful compromise between sincerity, resistance to gratuitous hurt, and encouraging good feeling in another. The benevolent lie is just pandering, indifferent to truth" (12). I think, however, that this insight is better captured by the view that I outline in section 4 of this chapter.

3.5 Ability to continue productive exchange

Alan Strudler (2010) suggests that there is the following important difference between lies and mere misleadings: once a lie has been revealed as such, trust collapses and further productive conversation becomes impossible. However, once a mere misleading has been revealed as such, productive conversation remains possible, despite a reduction in trust (one ceases to trust what is implicated, while continuing to trust what is said). He supports this with examples contrasting misleading with lying in a real estate negotiation, and what he says seems right for this case.

I am not, however, convinced that Strudler's claims are *generally* true of lies and misleadings. The first reason is that the revealing of lies does not always result in the total collapse of trust that it might cause in a negotiation. Here's just one example of the sort of thing that does in fact happen quite a lot.

A: How's your business going?
B: Excellent—we have lots of clients.
A: Really? Mine has dried up.
B: Well, actually, mine's dried up too. I was just afraid to say it.

Interestingly, the conversation between A and B is likely to improve and become *more trusting* once B's initial lie has been admitted. Before this it would in all likelihood have been stilted and brief.

The next problem with Strudler's claims is that revealing that someone has been misleading *can* in fact have a devastating effect on trust. One sort of case he discusses: cases in which the breach of trust by misleading is so vast that it could not be made worse by taking the form of a lie (the case of Charla and Dave or that of George and Frieda could be understood in this way). But this can also happen with very minor deceptions. Imagine that you are Beau, and the conversation mentioned earlier takes place.

Amanda: Where does the visiting speaker want to go to dinner, the Thai restaurant or the Ethiopian?
Beau: She says she likes Ethiopian.

Suppose now that it's revealed that Beau has very much misled Amanda: the speaker did say she likes Ethiopian, but she went on to say that she'd really like a change from it, having eaten Ethiopian for the last five nights. Moreover, Beau heard this and had not forgotten it. It seems to me that it would be very difficult to continue trusting productive conversation with someone who chose to be so perversely misleading, at least unless some good reason for the misleading could be offered.

So I don't think the contrast Strudler sketches is nearly as clear as he makes it out to be. Moreover, his central cases of deception in a real estate negotiation can easily be seen as the sort of special case that I will discuss in section 4.3.

3.6 Kant/Adler: inference and responsibility

Jonathan Adler (1997) has a different view from MacIntyre's regarding Kant's reason for morally distinguishing lying and mere misleading.

> The underlying idea is, presumably, that each individual is a rational, autonomous being and so fully responsible for the inferences he draws, just as he is for his acts. It is [misleading], but not lies, that require mistaken inferences and so are the hearer's responsibility. (444)

The victim of a misleading bears partial responsibility for her false belief; because responsibility for the false belief is shared in this way, the misleading speaker is not as culpable as the liar. After all, the misleader is only partly responsible for a deception, and the liar is fully responsible. Why is the misled audience partly responsible for her false belief? Because, the thought goes, she had to make an inference to get to it. In the case of successful lying, *a speaker says that P and their audience believes them*, thereby arriving at the false belief that P. In the case of successful misleading, *a speaker says that P, and the audience infers that Q from the speaker's utterance, thereby arriving at the false belief that Q*. In the lying case, then, all that the audience does is to believe the speaker. In the misleading case, the audience makes an inference and then forms the belief that what she has inferred is true. The audience, then, *does more* in the misleading case. The fact that she does more grounds the thought that she is *more responsible* for the belief that she arrives at.[16]

It seems not unreasonable to suppose that a thought like this is behind the line-drawing that I have found so puzzling. Here's the general idea: what is said is what the audience gets to automatically, without any inference. Anything beyond that is a matter of the audience's own inference. The speaker, then, is fully responsible for the audience believing

---

[16] This idea is endorsed by Stuart Green (2001: 166–7), as a part of his grounding for the Caveat Auditor principle, which I've already discussed above. Adler himself rejects the account for the same reason that he rejects Chisholm and Feehan's—that when a misleading is accomplished by implicature, it is *invited* by the speaker and so it is something for which the speaker is responsible. I think this objection succeeds in showing that the speaker bears some responsibility for a misleading by implicature. But it is not a full response to the view which assigns the audience partial responsibility on the basis of their inferences, since that view need not absolve the speaker of *all* responsibility.

what is said—this is what follows automatically from the speaker saying it, and the speaker knows this. But anything beyond this is at least partly up to the audience—it's not automatic, and it requires an inference that the audience can make or not make, as they choose. So it makes sense for a speaker's duties to end at what is said, as Kant suggests. Similarly, one can see this motivating Chisholm and Feehan's thoughts as well. We can see how an audience might have a right to expect that what is said is true, but how could an audience have a right to expect that the inferences *they make* are true? Insisting that misleading is a matter of audience inferences while successful lying is not seems a promising way, then, to ground a moral distinction between lying and misleading.

The problem with this, however, is that it overestimates the role of inference in being misled. In some of the cleverest cases of misleading, the audience immediately grasps the false claim that's conveyed, rather than inferring it from what is said. Take the case, for example, of my utterance of (7), despite my knowledge that Amada and Beau's marriage came after their children:

(7)   Amanda and Beau got married and had children.

Quite plausibly (see e.g. Grice 1989: 31) in this sort of case, the audience will immediately arrive at (8) as an interpretation of my utterance, without the need to work it out inferentially:

(8)   Amanda and Beau got married and then had children.

Nonetheless, my utterance of (7) seems very clearly to be a case of misleading rather than lying. If (8) is immediately arrived at, then this is a case where inferences on the part of the audience cannot be invoked in order to claim shared responsibility for the false belief.[17]

One might respond to this by questioning whether it is really right that no inference is involved in getting from the uttered sentence (7) to the interpretation captured by (8). After all, not all of our psychological

---

[17] Another case where the proposition conveyed is arrived at immediately, rather than by conscious inference, is Clinton's "There is no improper relationship". As noted earlier, listeners initially took this to be a full and timeless denial. It was only later that people began to notice the careful phrasing, and that Clinton had not said there never was a relationship. If listeners had first considered the exclusively present-tense denial, then inferred to the timeless denial, this would not have happened: the moment one realizes that Clinton has made only a present-tense denial, one becomes suspicious enough not to infer more.

processing is immediately accessible to us—it is very likely, in fact, that unconscious inferences are involved in this sort of processing.

In order for such unconscious inferences to ground a moral distinction between lying and misleading, however, it would need to be the case that they are not involved in the process by which the audience arrives at what is said. The idea would be that what is said can be automatically read off an utterance, without any need for inferences during processing. But this is a tremendously unrealistic picture. To take just one example, audiences must make inferences, relying on contextual cues, to work out the references of utterances of demonstrative terms like 'he' or 'that'. Sometimes this will even require *conscious* inference, as when an audience thinks to herself, *who does she mean by 'he'?*, then notices the speaker's pointing finger. Even more frequently, unconscious inferences will be involved. So we cannot ground a moral distinction between lying and misleading in any claim that only one of these involves audience inferences.

3.7 A subtler inference view?[18]

One might suggest that I have been too quick to dismiss the idea that something about the inferences involved in cases of lying and misleading could lead to differences in responsibility that could support the claim that lying is worse than merely misleading. Here's a different, subtler version of the view:

The inferences involved in working out the referents of indexicals are *mandatory* in an important way: without them, the audience will not be able to arrive at a truth-evaluable content for the speaker's utterance. If the audience gets to a false belief simply through working out what the speaker said (as in the case of a lie), they will have done so solely through mandatory inferences. But if they are merely misled, then they get to a false belief by engaging in some *non-mandatory* inferences. These inferences were not needed to get to a truth-evaluable content, because the audience could have carefully attended just to what was said. If they had done this, they would not have ended up with false beliefs. Thus, the audience bears partial responsibility for what occurs in a case of mere misleading. This is why lying is worse: the speaker bears all the responsibility for the outcome of the lie, but only partial responsibility for the outcome of the misleading utterance.

We have already noted one problem for this view: that in many cases of misleading, working out a conversational implicature is not optional, but

---

[18] I am grateful to Elisabeth Camp for suggesting this view to me.

required in order to understand the speaker as cooperative. Still, we can see that this is a different sort of requirement from the requirement to arrive at a truth-evaluable content. So let's set this worry aside. I think there is a more important problem with this way of justifying a moral distinction.

It is admittedly very appealing to suppose that a sharing of responsibility for the false belief might make misleading less morally problematic than lying. But it seems to me this view is seriously mistaken, and for quite a fundamental reason: being partly causally responsible for a wrong done to one does nothing to alter the nature of that wrong. To see this, compare the following two cases:

- Careful Victim: the careful mugging victim walks only through well-lit areas of town that he has been told are safe, and always keeps his wallet securely tucked into an inside jacket pocket. Nonetheless he is mugged.
- Reckless Victim: the reckless mugging victim walks through parts of town that he knows to be poorly lit and dangerous, with his bulging wallet clearly visible in his back pocket. He is mugged.

Reckless Victim, we would think, bears some responsibility for his mugging, while Careful Victim does not. This affects the way that we think about each of these people. But, it seems to me, it does nothing at all to affect the way that we think about the muggings. Both acts of mugging are equally wrong. Nor does it affect the way that we think about the muggers—even if we imagine that the mugger in the bad part of town carefully confines his efforts to the bad part of town, telling himself that what he does is a little bit better because he's only mugging people who are reckless.

Suppose we grant that the misleader's victim is partially responsible for her false belief in a way that the liar's victim is not partially responsible for hers. The misleader's victim could have carefully attended only to what was said, rather than inferring to something beyond that, just as Reckless Victim could have stuck to safe, well-lit parts of town. They each did something a bit riskier, and in each case it had bad consequences for them. But just as this fact does nothing to diminish the wrongness of the mugging, it similarly does nothing to diminish the wrongness of the deception. Being partially responsible for a wrong done to one does nothing to mitigate that wrong. Nor does it do anything to mitigate the blameworthiness of the wrongdoer. And this is the case even if the wrongdoer only preys on those who are reckless in some way. A mugger who only plies his trade in bad parts of town is no more laudable than one who works in good parts of town as well. Similarly for a deceiver who never lies, always deceiving only those reckless enough to infer to something beyond what has been said. The partial causal responsibility of a victim does not in any way affect the wrongness of what is done to them.

Why, then, should we find it so natural to think otherwise? The answer, it seems to me, is that we're quite bad at thinking about cases of this sort. The mugging case is a clear one, for which what I've suggested would, I think, meet with near-universal agreement. But to alter intuitions all we need to do is to change the crime from mugging to rape. It is, unfortunately, extremely common to find people who hold the view that e.g. the rape of a woman who knowingly walks through a bad part of town is less bad than the rape of a woman who confines herself to areas that are supposedly safe.[19] It seems likely that street crime, including rape, is more common in bad parts of town, and therefore that one who goes into bad parts of town raises the odds that she will be victimized. If this is right, one might argue that a woman who walks through a bad part of town bears partial *causal* responsibility for her rape, just as Reckless Victim bears partial *causal* responsibility for his mugging. But in both cases it would be an enormous mistake to move from this to a claim of moral responsibility or to a mitigation of the wrongness of the crime.

I don't know why it is that we find it so natural to suppose that—*in some cases*—a victim's causal partial responsibility for their fate means that what has been done to them is less wrong. But this apparently natural view seems to me to be one that we should firmly reject. Once we reject this view, we have no reason to suppose that differing levels of responsibility for inferences in cases of lying and misleading might render misleading morally preferable to lying.

3.8 Adler: our need for deception

Jonathan Adler (1997) offers an intriguing and original justification for the moral preference for misleading over lying. He points out that we have a

---

[19] The rape example is a complex one, so much so that I am hesitant to use it here. In many people's responses to rape there are a large number of other factors involved: belief in rape myths (e.g. that women really want to be raped), misogyny, suspicion of victim testimony, etc. Yet it still seems to me likely that one factor is at least sometimes confusion regarding the relationships between partial causal responsibility, moral responsibility, blame, and wrongness.

legitimate need, sometimes, to deceive. Key examples he offers include cases of discretion or tact. But one could also make this point by considering cases of an even more pressing need, such as the need to deceive the murderer at the door. This need of ours is what generates a norm of conversation involving a lesser demand of truthfulness for information that is merely conveyed, rather than said; and this norm "acquires moral force".

So a norm corresponding to the lessened demands of truthfulness for implicatures would be desirable for all. Such a norm of conversation acquires moral force. Given the previously mentioned "strains of commitment" generated by the numerous situations pressuring us to deceive, it is rational for each of us to want cooperative accommodation with others. The difference in demands of truthfulness for [what is said] compared to implicatures provides a salient rationale for a corresponding ethical norm. For the difference is an endorsed mutual expectation under which our contributions are offered and accepted, or occasionally challenged. (451)

This suggestion has, to my mind, a great deal of intuitive appeal. It would be immensely attractive to find a way of getting from our need for occasional deception to a morally significant lying–misleading distinction. But I don't see a good way of doing this. The problem is that there is another norm that would address our needs much more clearly and completely: a lessened demand for truthfulness when there is genuinely good reason to deceive. Again, I think an analogy may be useful. It is commonly accepted that violence is bad, but that we have an occasional legitimate need to commit violent acts, for example in self-defence or in defence of someone else. (This seems to me analogous to our view that deception is wrong, but that we have an occasional legitimate need to deceive.) And there is indeed have a commonly accepted view that some violence is morally acceptable. But we differentiate the morally acceptable violence from the morally unacceptable violence not by focusing on method of violence (knife, gun, fist, kick, etc.) but instead on the occasion for violence (e.g. self-defence or without provocation). This would be by far the more natural way to deal with the situation concerning deception: differentiate between permissible and impermissible deceptions according to their purpose—rather than according to their method. (Differentiating between them on the basis of method seems analogous to the view that, say, punching is better than kicking.)[20] A norm focused on *method* of deception is utterly mysterious.

---

[20] We do differentiate between e.g. using a gun and using a fist. But presumably that is because the outcome is so different in the two cases, which it is not with lying vs. misleading.

One might respond to this that a norm focused on method of deception makes sense, given the expectations that are in place. Everybody knows that there is lessened demand for truthfulness in what is conversationally implicated than in what is said. As a result, people should know to be cautious about believing what is merely conveyed, and if they are not cautious they share some of the blame for their deception. But this argument seems to depend on the idea that a victim's partial causal responsibility reduces the wrongness of what is done to them. And I have already argued against this.

4 An alternative

The alternative picture I am proposing here rejects a general moral preference for misleading over lying, even a defeasible one. It agrees with the first tradition mentioned at the start of this chapter that there simply is no defensible moral preference of this sort. Nonetheless, it recognizes—and, I think, respects—the importance of the lying–misleading distinction to the moral psychology of so many of us.

4.1 *Evaluating acts and evaluating persons*

On this picture, the moral significance of the lying–misleading distinction is not simply a matter of whether (in general, all else being equal) mere misleading is morally better than lying. The answer to this question is a simple 'no'. But this is not all that matters. We're not simply mistaken in our moral judgements about instances of lying and misleading—we're getting something right as well, at least when it comes to many particular cases. My suggestion is that when we consider the morality of particular acts, as we do when presented with cases of lying and misleading, we actually think about more than just the morality of the acts. As far as the acts go, misleading is not morally better than lying.[21] But when we're reflecting on the morality of the *acts*, we're often reflecting as well on the virtuousness of the *actor*—without always being aware that we are doing this. And decisions about lying and misleading may be genuinely (not just apparently) morally revealing about the character of the actor.

---

[21] As noted earlier, this is not to deny that they are different sorts of acts. It's simply a denial that one is morally superior to the other.

To see what all this comes to, it helps to look again at the case of the dying woman who asks about her son's welfare. As I presented the example, I asked you to think about whether you would consider it better to mislead the woman with (1) or to lie to her with (2).

(1) I saw him yesterday and he was happy and healthy.
(2) He's happy and healthy.

If you are like most people, you judged that it would be morally better to utter (1) rather than (2). My suggestion here is that this judgement is false: uttering (1) is no better than uttering (2), as both are intentional deceptions of the old woman about exactly the same thing and with the same motivation. Why, then, did you think otherwise?

One obvious reason that we think otherwise is, of course, that we believe (falsely, according to me) that acts of misleading are better than acts of lying. No shock, then, that we judge it to be better to mislead the old woman than to lie to her. But this isn't the whole story, and we can see this by considering a variant on the example. Imagine now that I am not at all concerned with the woman's happiness. However, I am the beneficiary of her son's will. If he remains her heir, I know that I will inherit her fortune. If she learns that he is dead, however, she will change her will and I will not inherit her fortune. I'm a little worried, though, that my claim to the fortune could be legally questioned if it emerges that I've lied. So I utter (1) when she asks about her son's health—because it is not a lie. When we think about this case, I think, our judgements are quite different. I think we're *far* less likely to have the intuition that I do something morally better by uttering (1) than I would have done by uttering (2). So our judgements aren't just determined by our false conviction that acts of lying are worse than acts of misleading.

My suggestion is that when we think about such cases, we often muddle together our thoughts about the morality of the acts and our thoughts about the morality of the agents—and that the latter often affects our judgements of the former. I think we're absolutely right to suppose that decisions to lie or mislead are often morally revealing about agents—even though we're wrong when we take this to mean that one sort of act is morally better than the other.

In thinking about the agents involved, we really do latch on to something morally significant. When you think about the first, benevolent version of the old woman example, you probably imagine yourself feeling torn by the desire to avoid causing the woman pointless pain, and the desire not to deceive. Feeling torn in this way, you choose the carefully crafted (1) rather than the outright lie (2). Even though it's a deception (which you probably feel guilty about), it is, you think (or at least hope), a morally better sort of deception. You've failed in your desire not to deceive, but at least you *had* that desire, and you felt moved by it. And you did something which you thought made your deception a little bit less bad than it otherwise would have been. When we try to imagine the kind of person who would choose (2), it is very likely that we imagine someone who really doesn't care about deceiving the woman. And this seems like a worse person. These are moral judgements. The choice between lying and misleading is (often, anyway) one that reveals something of genuine moral significance.

This alternative picture allows us to make sense of the cases in which we judge acts of misleading *not* to be morally superior to acts of lying. Our judgements in these cases, quite obviously, can't be explained as resulting from our belief that acts of misleading are morally superior to acts of lying. But they can be explained as really resulting from our judgements of agents. In the greedy speaker version of the dying woman, the choice to mislead reveals nothing that is at all laudable. (Indeed, it reveals something quite bad about them.) We're not, then, moved to think the act is morally better by our judgement of the agent. We can also make sense of the counter-examples to (M) that I presented at the start of this chapter. Charla's choice to mislead Dave about her HIV status reveals nothing at all that is admirable about her, so we don't feel at all tempted to judge that this misleading is morally superior to lying. Similarly for the cook who murderously misleads about the content of his food. I think we doubt that such people could possibly have good motivations for their choices to mislead rather than to lie. And if they genuinely think that what they do is improved by the fact that they are misleading rather than lying, this seems like a culpable igno-rance about what is morally significant. Similarly, for some of us anyway, the person who tries hard to mislead the murderer rather than lie to them reveals that her priorities are all wrong: she should care far more about preventing murder than about avoiding a lie. For others, the effort to *both* prevent murder and avoid lying will seem noble. In all these cases, we can best make sense of our judgements if we realize that we are judging *what the acts reveal about the people doing them*, rather than the morality of the acts themselves.

This also helps us to make a sense of a certain partisan tinge to some of our judgements. Those who think (as I do) that Bill Clinton was unfairly persecuted for his personal life as part of a (vast) right-wing conspiracy do tend to judge that he did something morally better by uttering (9) in an interview than he would have done by uttering (10).

(9) There is no improper relationship.

(10) There was no improper relationship.

But those who think badly of Clinton generally deny that (9) was a morally better choice than (10) would have been. Sometimes, they even seem to think it was a morally worse one. This difference now makes sense. People like me take Clinton's choice of (9) to be a sensible way of dealing with the unfair position that he was put in. We think that Clinton did not want to lie but also wanted to evade the harm that could come from this persecution, and we took this to be a wholly reasonable response to the situation he found himself in. If he had simply lied with (10) that would have showed a lack of concern about deceit. So Clinton's (9) revealed something good about him, according to Democratic partisans like me. But for those who hate Clinton, things are different. For these people, the choice of (9) rather than (10) revealed only a disreputable sneakiness, a desire to evade the accountability that might come if he was caught in a lie. If anything, on this view, this choice revealed something bad about Clinton. Our judgements of Clinton's choice between (9) and (10) are deeply infected by our judgements of Clinton's character. And this is something that makes perfect sense on the picture presented here.

Similar considerations arise with the case of Judith Miller, the *New York Times* reporter who went to jail for her refusal to reveal the source who told her various things relevant to the Valerie Plame investigation. Miller was apparently asked by her source, Vice Presidential Chief of Staff Scooter Libby, to identify him only as "a former Hill staffer". She says that she "agreed to the new ground rules because I knew that Mr Libby had once worked on Capitol Hill" (Kamen 2005). What Miller agreed to do was to describe Libby in a truthful but misleading way. If she had said "A former Hill staffer told me this", she would have misled while avoiding lying.[22] And avoidance of lying clearly mattered to her: she agreed *because* she knew that the description was true of Libby. Did this make the

---

[22] In Kamen's rather wonderful article, he also notes that by Miller's standard it would be correct to describe Bush's utterances as those of a 'a cheerleader', Condoleezza Rice's as those of a 'football fan', and Dick Cheney's as those of an 'Ivy League dropout'.

utterance any better than it would have been if it had been a lie? Some might argue that she showed an honourable journalistic desire to protect her sources coupled with an honourable journalistic desire to not utter falsehoods—so the choice to carefully mislead showed only good things about her. Others might argue that she showed a reprehensible willingness to facilitate some of the Bush administration's most despicable acts, coupled with a desire for deniability—so the choice showed only bad things about her. On the view suggested here, the moral significance of Miller's choice to mislead but not to lie is to be found wholly in its relevance to evaluations of her overall character—and this relevance will vary tremendously.

This view even allows us to make sense of cases in which a choice to mislead is judged as *worse* than a choice to lie. David Runciman (2006) made such a judgement regarding certain utterances of Gordon Brown's, made when Brown was not yet Prime Minister. The context for Brown's remarks was a Labour Party Conference, at which all in attendance knew that Brown and Blair disliked each other, and that Brown was desperate for Blair to finally step aside and hand him the Prime Minister's job.

What Brown claimed in his speech was that it had been a privilege to serve under Tony Blair as prime minister. This was too much for Cherie [Blair] to stomach, but strictly speaking it wasn't a lie, since every chancellor holds office on the sufferance of the prime minister, and for Blair to have put up with Brown for so long was indeed quite an honour. What's more, I have a horrible feeling that Brown said it because he knew it wasn't technically untrue, and his own sense of probity required that whatever he said to smooth over his differences with Blair shouldn't be a brazen falsehood. Brown is not a born liar: he is, as we keep being reminded, a son of the manse, which, if it means anything, means that. But by not actually lying, Brown came across as something worse, a man who was happy to conceal the true state of his feelings.

Runciman's thought, it seems to me, is that by misleading rather than lying Brown took himself to be doing something perfectly acceptable ("happy to conceal the true state of his feelings"). If he had lied, Brown would have had to face up to the reality of what he was doing—deceiving. By misleading, Brown could convince himself that he wasn't doing anything wrong. And so Runciman's view is that Brown's choice to mislead is more contemptible than a choice to lie would be.

4.2 Why are lying/misleading choices morally revealing?

I haven't yet said anything about why the choice to lie or mislead may be morally revealing about a person's character. I'll begin to rectify this by making it clear that I don't think there is something special about this choice that makes it revealing in a way that no other choices are. I do, however, think there is something interesting about it.

Some choices have a tendency to be revealing about people's moral characters. In general, these are choices between options where one is morally better than another: I can help the person I see lying on the sidewalk, I can simply step over them, or I can say something abusive to them. It's not hard to see how my choice between these options reveals something morally significant about me. Other choices are not morally significant. Obvious cases include my choice of whether to wear the socks with purple toes or the socks with orange toes, both of which are in the sock drawer in front of me. This choice isn't morally significant because the options aren't morally different from each other.

What's interesting about the case of choices between lying and misleading is that it seems plausible to suppose that such choices will often be morally revealing; and yet, if I am right, one is *not* morally better than the other. Nothing hangs, morally, on whether the old woman is deceived by a lie or a carefully constructed misleading. So perhaps it's puzzling that my choice between these options could be morally revealing. It's worth noting briefly that there's nothing at all morally puzzling about the fact that *we tend to believe* these choices to be morally revealing, if we're among the many people who falsely believe that lying is morally worse than merely misleading. If we are like this, then these are choices between actions where we falsely take one to be morally better that the other; of course *we think* such choices are morally revealing. The puzzle is why such choices should be *genuinely* morally revealing, even if one action isn't morally superior to the other.

4.2.1 Abnormal contexts In many cases, there is a simple answer to this apparent puzzle: the reason that many choices to lie or mislead are likely to be genuinely revealing is that most of us are ignorant of the fact (if I'm right) that misleading is not morally preferable to lying. Cheshire Calhoun's distinction between *normal* and *abnormal* moral contexts is helpful here. Normal moral contexts are contexts in which "the sharing of moral knowledge allows us to assume that most rational, reflective people could come to correct judgments about which courses of action would be right, wrong, or controversial" (1989: 395). In normal contexts, moral ignorance will be "ignorance of what the moral community in general knows. This is why . . . it would . . . take a very special story for 'I didn't know that polluting public waterways is wrong' . . . to be an acceptable excuse" (395).[23] In abnormal moral contexts, there are moral truths known only to a small group. My suggestion is that—if I'm right that misleading isn't morally preferable to lying—we're in an abnormal context when it comes to the lying–misleading distinction. The truth about this distinction—that acts of lying aren't morally worse than acts of misleading—is not known to most people. Most people think that it is morally better to mislead than to lie. It's no surprise, then, that choices to lie or mislead are often morally revealing: they are choices between options where one is genuinely believed to be morally superior to the other.

So far, I've been arguing that one reason choices between lying and misleading are morally revealing is that they're often based on a false belief that misleading is morally better than lying. This gives rise to two questions: (1) Do all false beliefs about morality have this sort of effect on our judgements? And (2) What about cases where the choice is clearly *not* based on such a false belief?

4.2.2 Other false beliefs about morality   I've suggested, above, that agents' false belief that lying is worse than merely misleading helps to make their choices to mislead rather than lie *genuinely* morally revealing ones. The question arises, then, what I should say about cases where such a choice is based on a different sort of false belief. Take, for example, the belief that lies of precisely seven words are morally superior to other lies, and imagine an agent who carefully lives by this rule, planning out his seven-word lies so as to engage in morally better actions. Is the choice to lie in seven-word utterances a genuinely morally revealing one?[24]

I think this choice is genuinely morally revealing, but not in the same way as the choice to mislead rather than to lie. The reason is that we are

---

[23] The example is Calhoun's. Jonathan Adler has pointed out to me that one could raise doubts about how widely known this fact is. It seems to me, however, that even though there *is* a lot of pollution of public waterways going on, this is due not to moral ignorance but to lack of concern for this moral issue.

[24] I'm grateful to Collin O'Neill for suggesting an example of this sort.

not in an abnormal context with respect to the seven-word lie rule. There is ample evidence available to any reasonable agent that this is not a sensible moral rule. Nobody else follows this rule, and the agent surely knows this. Nor is anybody else aware of this rule. As a result, lies with seven-words very clearly function in exactly the same way in the world as other lies. Insisting that one believes seven-word lies are morally superior is quite a bit like insisting that one doesn't know that polluting public waterways is wrong. The false moral belief is a culpable one, because a reasonable agent would easily see that it's false. This is morally revealing because it does reveal something about the agent's moral thinking: it reveals a culpably false moral belief. Because we're not in an abnormal context with respect to seven-word lies, an agent does not do anything better by using lies of only seven words—and their moral ignorance is blameworthy in and of itself.

4.2.3 Choices not based on false belief about lying–misleading distinction Not all choices to mislead rather than to lie are based on the false belief that misleading is morally superior to lying. We will consider two sorts of choices not based on this belief.

4.2.3.1 CHOICES BASED ON DIFFERENT DESIRES

Some choices to mislead rather than to lie are ones where the choice is based not on a desire to do something morally better, but instead on a different desire. Some such choices, for example, are based simply on a desire for deniability. In a case like this, we obviously won't judge the agent do be doing something morally laudable by misleading rather than lying. Instead, we will judge them to be doing something deeply morally problematic—the agent is doing something wrong, and choosing a way of doing it that they think will help them to evade blame from others. It is no surprise that this should be morally revealing, and in a negative way.

4.2.3.2 CHOICES OF THOSE IN THE KNOW

If I am right in what I have argued here, there is (in general) nothing morally better about carrying out some particular attempted deception by way of a deliberately misleading utterance rather than a lie. Most of us don't know this yet. But some of us do. I do, for example (assuming that I'm right). So what happens when I am faced with a desire to deceive? I'd like to say this never happens, but of course that's not true. I wish I could also say that I no longer feel any pull to construct a carefully misleading utterance rather than simply utter a lie. But again, this isn't true: when I think about that dying woman, I still feel a desire to choose the misleading response rather than the lie. The difference is that I'm no longer convinced that this choice actually makes any moral difference. And when I do make such a choice in real life (it happens, I admit it), I no longer take comfort in the confidence that what I've done is a little less bad than it otherwise would have been. Why, then, do I still do this? One answer is surely 'habit'—this is a habit that most of us acquire quite early in childhood, and such habits are hard to break. Another, in my case, is a lack of confidence in my philosophical views. Convincing as I find my arguments, I'm never all *that* sure of my philosophical views. The decision to mislead rather than lie, in my case, can be seen as based on the thought that *maybe* misleading is better than lying after all—so I should choose it just in case.[25] Alternatively, and less flatteringly, it could be simply hypocrisy or self-deception (in the latter case, I might be deceiving myself into feeling less guilt than is appropriate.)

How should we morally assess what I do when I choose to mislead rather than lie, despite my belief that misleading is not better than lying? I'm not sure. Perhaps this verdict will depend on whether we view it as hypocrisy (since I think this choice is not a morally better one); or an epistemically modest hedging of bets (since I'm not so certain that I'm right); or a self-deceived effort to avoid feelings of guilt. But one thing does seem clear to me: deception was easier on my conscience before I arrived at the view I've defended in this chapter. Then, I did find it comforting to find a way to mislead rather than to lie. That comfort is no longer available to me.[26]

4.3 Special contexts

But the truth, I think, is even more complicated than the admittedly already complicated picture sketched above. The truth is also that there are certain special contexts in which misleading *is* morally worse than lying. Moreover, it is not completely straightforward to decide which contexts are like this. We'll begin with clear cases, then look at some murkier ones.

---

[25] The reasoning here bears certain similarities to that involved in Pascal's Wager.

[26] I extend my apologies to any readers convinced by my argument—deception is likely to become harder on your consciences as well.

4.3.1 Legal contexts, and other possibly similar ones

4.3.1.1 LEGAL CONTEXTS

Under US law, perjury requires the saying of something false—merely conveying a falsehood is insufficient. This alone is not enough to ground a moral distinction in courtroom contexts—the law need not coincide with morality, after all. But it can be compellingly argued (as Solan and Tiersma (2005) have done) that the law is right to put the emphasis that it does on what is said—because of distinctive features of courtroom contexts—at least within an adversarial legal system like the US one.

To see this, consider the classic case of *Bronston* v. *United States*. Samuel Bronston had both personal and company bank accounts in several countries. At his company's bankruptcy hearing, the following exchange took place between Bronston and a lawyer (Solan and Tiersma: 213):

Lawyer: Do you have any bank accounts in Swiss banks, Mr Bronston?
Bronston: No, Sir.
Lawyer: Have you ever?
Bronston: The company had an account there for about six months, in Zurich.

Because Bronston himself had earlier had a large personal bank account in Switzerland, he was charged with perjury. The basis of the perjury charge was that, while his second utterance above was literally true, it was deeply misleading in that it conveyed that Bronson had never had a personal Swiss bank account. The eventual verdict by the US Supreme Court was that a merely misleading statement is not perjury. Solan and Tiersma, in their analysis of this verdict, argue convincingly that this was the right ruling, both legally and morally. In a courtroom, a witness is required to answer the questions that a lawyer puts to them. If either of the lawyers in an adversarial system is not satisfied with their answers, it is the lawyer's job to pursue the questions further. The lawyers are trained professionals, well versed in these matters. It is very much the lawyer's job to notice that a witness is not answering the question asked, and to force them to answer the right question. As a result, the lawyer questioning Bronston had a responsibility to press Bronston further on his misleading statement.

[T]he message of the Supreme Court in Bronston is that errors, vagueness, ambiguity, and lack of responsiveness ought to be corrected during the questioning process, not by prosecuting the witness for perjury after the fact. (2005: 215–16)

There is a clear division of responsibilities in a courtroom, with the legal professionals (lawyer and judge) responsible for making sure that all responses are complete and appropriate, and fully disambiguated and recorded. Because of this, the Kantian view discussed earlier makes a kind of sense for courtrooms that is hard to credit more broadly:

> my duty is to assert [in our terms, say] only what is true and the mistaken inferences which others may draw from what I say or what I do are, in some cases at least, not my responsibility, but theirs. (MacIntyre 1994: 337)

This seems right, when it comes to courtroom testimony, for the reasons outlined above.

Interestingly, the law makes a sharp distinction between courtroom contexts and other ones, when it comes to the importance of literal meaning. The law on threats treats indirect threats in the same way that it treats direct ones. Take the case of a criminal who tells witnesses to a crime, "if they say anything to the police, 'something is going to happen to them'" (Solan and Tiersma 2005). Taken literally this is simply an obvious truth. Something will happen to the witnesses if they talk to the police, just as something will happen to them if they don't. In fact, many things will happen to them. Perhaps they'll meet the love of their lives, perhaps they'll get rained on, perhaps they'll be served some really bad coffee, perhaps they'll pass the big exam next week, perhaps they'll have to deal with a leaky tap . . . But pointing this out would be no defence. Taken in context, a threat is clearly meant and understood, and it does not matter that this threat is not literally said.[27]

A key reason for drawing the distinction between courtroom contexts and threats in ordinary life is that, as we've noted, in the courtroom there are highly trained lawyers whose job it is to get clear and unequivocal statements out of those testifying. If something is left as implied rather than spelled out, it is to a significant degree the fault of the lawyers who fail to ask follow-up questions. No such thing is true in ordinary life when we are being threatened. We (most of us, anyway) do not employ highly trained people to travel around with us and make sure that everyone we speak to has made themselves wholly explicit. Moreover (and perhaps more to the

---

[27] Solan and Tiersma (2005) do note that case law is not wholly consistent on this, citing a case in which a rapist's utterance, "I don't want to hurt you" was not held to be a threat. They view this verdict as one that resulted from a patriarchal bias, and hold that the court would have ruled differently in a case other than a rape one.

point), when we are threatened we are thereby placed in a position of lessened power relative to the person who has threatened us. We are often frightened, and not in a position to try to extract precise language (even if we wanted to). So if a court is to take seriously the harm done by threats, and their impact on us, it needs to focus not on what is literally said but instead on what is conveyed by the utterance in context. Speech on the witness stand is a special, and different sort of speech. The witness stand offers a very different sort of context, in which there is very good reason for placing a significant emphasis on the distinction between what is strictly speaking said and what is otherwise communicated.[28]

4.3.1.2 RELATED CONTEXTS

This does not mean, however, that the witness stand is the only context like this. Quite plausibly political interviews (at least some of them) may be relevantly like courtrooms. Consider, again, Bill Clinton's utterance of (9), in response to the interviewer's question, "Did you have an improper relationship with Ms Lewinsky?"

(9)   There is no improper relationship.
(9*)   There was no improper relationship.

Earlier, in considering Bill Clinton's choice to utter (9) rather than (9*), I focused on the fact that our evaluation of his act may be affected by what the act reveals about Clinton as an agent. Now, however, I want to examine the possibility that Clinton's act of misleading may genuinely have been better than a lie would have been. An interview with a politician who is the subject of breaking scandal is quite an adversarial context. The interviewer will (or at least should) be fully aware that their interviewee will attempt evasion. It is the interviewer's job to press the interviewee to answer the questions put to them, and to make sure that

---

[28] Another sort of legal context also provides an exception. Larry Solan writes in his 2010 that lawyers "are required to tell the truth in the context of legal proceedings. At the same time, they are insincere in that they routinely present themselves as honest purveyors of the truth, whereas they have told only the most self-serving part of the story". These rules, which are quite explicit, require lawyers not to lie during legal proceedings but allow them to mislead. Because of these rules, it is better for lawyers to mislead than to lie. After all, a lawyer who lies is breaking a rule that he has implicitly agreed to by practising law in knowledge of these rules. A lawyer who misleads is following the rules of his profession. Indeed, as Solan points out, lawyers are often taught that misleading may sometimes be a professional obligation.

they don't get away with a potentially misleading answer. Perhaps it's reasonable, then, to have the same sort of clear division of responsibilities in these interviews that there is in a courtroom. It certainly doesn't seem unreasonable to me to suppose that it was the interviewer's job to make Clinton respond to his question, and that Clinton's job was only to avoid saying false things.

4.3.2 Explicit and less explicit agreements There are also other contexts in which misleading is in fact morally better than lying. Imagine, for example, that a couple decides to have an open relationship. They agree that they do not want to be told about each other's affairs, and that lying is forbidden. However, they know that it may be difficult to manage all this, so they also agree that mere misleading is perfectly acceptable. In this relationship, very clearly, misleading about one's affairs is morally preferable to lying about one's affairs. This is due to an explicit rule in place, and to the parties' agreement to follow this rule. To lie about one's affairs is to break the agreement; to merely mislead is to abide by the agreement. There is no puzzle about why the former should be morally preferable to the latter.

Explicit agreements offer us a very clear case. But there are also far less clear cases. Continuing on from the example above, a couple might have an unspoken but only hinted-at agreement like the one described. If both understand this agreement in the same way, I think the intuition that there is such an agreement is strong. As a result, it will seem quite right to say that misleading is morally better than lying in such a case.

Now imagine, though that one member of the couple takes there to be an implicit agreement of this sort and the other doesn't. In this case, there is no agreement—an agreement requires the parties to *agree*, after all. But our judgements will get a little tricky. Suppose that Gert genuinely takes there to be a non-explicit agreement between herself and Harry that affairs are fine, and misleading each other about affairs is fine, but lying about them is unacceptable. Harry, however, thinks that they have agreed to have affairs but neither lie nor mislead about them. Gert now misleads Harry about an affair. Has she done something better than what she would have done if she was lying? This is a very difficult question to answer. There is, in fact, no agreement, but Gert thinks that there is one. Perhaps the right answer is that Gert hasn't done anything better by choosing to mislead rather than to lie—but that her false belief that there was an agreement means that our overall evaluation of her will be more positive than it would have been if she had lied.

5 The complex alternative picture

The picture sketched in this chapter is a very complicated one, which both rejects and respects both traditions with which we began this chapter. The first tradition holds that method of deception is never a matter of moral significance: lying and misleading are equally bad or good, and the moral status of any particular deception depends on such things as its goal or its consequences. The second tradition holds that lying is always wrong, and that misleading is always better than lying (even if it isn't always morally acceptable). The view developed here firmly rejects both of these.

Against the second view, I maintain that misleading is *not* always better than lying. I showed this through an examination of cases in which misleading was not morally preferable to lying. Further, I argued that there does not seem to be any good justification even for a defeasible version of this view—on which misleading is, *except in certain special cases*, morally better than lying.

But I do not agree with the first tradition's claim that method of deception is never a matter of moral significance. I take method of deception to be moral significance in all of the following ways:

(1) Whether an agent chooses to lie or merely mislead can make an important difference to moral evaluations of an *agent*.

(2) In an adversarial context like a courtroom, misleading is morally better than lying.

(3) Where there is a prior agreement that misleading is to be preferred to lying, misleading is morally better than lying.

5

Some Interesting Cases

In the preceding chapters, I attempted to discern what notion of saying was needed for the lying–misleading distinction and to work out the moral significance of this distinction. This chapter puts the results of this investigation to work, showing how it is that they can shed some light on a range of tricky, interesting, or historically significant examples. We'll look, for instance, at various Jesuit doctrines about deception that brought the Catholic Church into disrepute—and led to Bill Clinton being called 'Jesuitical' for his carefully phrased utterances during the Monica Lewinsky sex scandal. And we'll look—rather extensively—at those utterances from Clinton. One reason for this is their importance to discussions of perjury law. But the more significant reason is that they help to show just how much can turn on distinctions like those discussed here—after all, Clinton was nearly removed from office over these issues. This chapter is intended to function not as a single sustained argument, but rather as a series of case studies. My hope is that together they show they value of an investigation like that I have undertaken in this book—one which draws on both ethics and philosophy of language—by shedding light on matters of significance both within philosophy and outside it.

1 Summary

Before we look at cases, it's probably a good idea to pause for a brief summary of what I've argued for in the previous chapters. As I discuss the cases, I'll be drawing on the conclusions that I drew in these chapters.

1.1 Lying

In Chapter 1, I argued that the understanding of lying needed for the lying–misleading distinction is the following:

Lying: If the speaker is not the victim of linguistic error/malapropism or using metaphor, hyperbole, or irony, then they lie iff (1) they say that P; (2) they believe P to be false;[1] (3) they take themself to be in a warranting context.

1.2 What is said

In Chapter 2, I argued that there does not seem to be any notion in the philosophy of language literature that can fulfil the role of saying for the lying–misleading distinction. The notion of saying I eventually arrived at in Chapter 3 is one on which contextually supplied material may only be a part of what is said by some utterance if condition (NTE) is met (and cashed out as indicated in Chapter 3, section 2.1):

(NTE) A putative contextual contribution to what is said is a part of what is said only if without this contextually supplied material, S would not have a truth-evaluable semantic content in C.

1.3 Moral significance

In Chapter 4, I argued that the distinction between lying and misleading does not have the moral significance so often assigned to it. Specifically, (M) is false (and also that there is no good justification for even a weakened version of (M)):

(M) Holding all else fixed, lying is morally worse than merely deliberately attempting to mislead; and successful lying is morally worse than merely deliberately misleading.

Nonetheless, I argued, the distinction frequently does have moral significance—because whether a person chooses to lie or mislead is often revealing of their moral character, and also because there are certain special contexts in which misleading is morally preferable to lying.

Now let's see how all this plays out over a range of examples.

2 Casuistical manoeuvres

2.1 The Doctrine of Mental Reservation

2.1.1 A brief description The Doctrine of Mental Reservation was a Casuist doctrine which held that in certain very special circumstances (e.g.

---

[1] Those thinking lies must be false would rephrase this as "they truly believe P to be false".

conditions of persecution or need to preserve confessional secrecy), certain special linguistic manoeuvres were permitted. The resulting utterances were not considered to be lies. For example, when asked by a persecutor, "Are you a priest?" a priest could avoid lying by uttering (1), while thinking to himself what is captured by (1*):

(1)   No, I am not a priest.
(1*) No, I am not a priest of Apollo.

A key bit of supporting evidence for this doctrine was its ability to explain the otherwise troubling fact that, according to scripture, Jesus (who a Christian would not want to see as a liar) claimed that he "'knew not the day nor the hour' of the Last Judgment" (Jonsen and Toulmin 1998: 196, 198). The problem is that (according to scripture) Jesus clearly did know this, since he was in fact the omniscient God. So proponents of the Doctrine of Mental Reservation suggested that what Jesus was really thinking when he uttered (2) was something like (2*).

(2)   I know not the day nor the hour of the Last Judgement.
(2*) I know not the day nor the hour of the Last Judgement, so that it may be revealed to you.

This Doctrine has not had many supporters through the ages, and was never universally accepted even by Jesuits. It became well enough known, however, that oaths were specifically written in such a way as to guard against it:

I do plainly and sincerely acknowledge and swear, according to these express words by me spoken and according to the plain and common sense and understanding of the same words, without any equivocation or secret reservation whatsoever. (Jonsen and Toulmin 1998: 210)[2]

Eventually, the doctrine brought the Catholic Church into such disrepute that it was condemned by Pope Innocent XI in 1679.[3] What can we say about it?

---

[2] Of course, as Chris Hookway and Roy Sorensen have pointed out to me this would be totally inefficacious. The user of mental reservation would merely need to add on a reservation like *about aardvarks*.

[3] Although the doctrine was condemned, it is still in use. A friend who worked in a Catholic hospital tells me that the nuns very deliberately make use of it in talking to patients. If a patient with a fever asked what his temperature was, the nun might say "normal", adding silently to herself "for a person in your condition". Some might want to treat this as exploitation of a contextually varying term—'normal', rather than a use of Mental

2.1.2 Analysis Mental reservation clearly does not count as lying under our definitions of 'lying', as applied with our understanding of what is said in mind. An initially plausible analysis is that mental reservation is a form of Expansion (disallowed under our understanding of saying)—but one on which the contextually supplied elements are not salient to the audience. One can also, however, raise questions about whether the contextually supplied elements are actually meant by the speaker. Bernard Williams argues that the speaker cannot genuinely believe that the audience will pick up on these contextually supplied elements, and that therefore they cannot genuinely be meant (2002: 104). If this is right—the contextually supplied material is neither genuinely meant nor salient—then even Constrained Theorists, who allow Expansion, would not allow *this* sort of Expansion. They would insist that the priest who utters (1) does *not* say what is captured by (1*). The view of saying defended in Chapter 3 would have the same result, even more directly—because Expansion is not permitted. The contextually supplied material in (1*) is not needed in order to arrive at a truth-evaluable semantic content, so it is not a part of what is said. So, the priest who utters (1) while thinking (1*) to himself has said something false.

But this is not, I think, what the priest takes himself to be doing. The priest believes that God hears his thoughts. For now, we'll assume that there is a God who does indeed hear the priest's thoughts. And, for the priest, God is a very important audience. The priest, it seems to me, is addressing two audiences, who have different perceptual capacities. What the priest says to his earthly audience is false, as described above. But what he says to God is *I am not a priest of Apollo*. And this is true. Interestingly, we get this result even on an Austere conception of saying, if we assume that God is hearing the priest's thoughts. So far as God is concerned, the priest *has* uttered the sentence "I am not a priest of Apollo".

This is a strange sort of case. It's one where a person simultaneously makes two different utterances, to two different audiences. Some analogies may help us here.

Reservation. But the fact that the nun emphasized the need to silently "say" additional words suggests that she was attempting to use Mental Reservation. I'll discuss another, more disturbing, recent use at the end of section 2.1.2.

(1) Imagine that I write "I am British" on a whiteboard at the same time that I say out loud "I am French". I know that I am speaking to two people, one who is blind and one who is deaf (and unable to lip-read). It's pretty clear in this case that I've said two things: I've said something true to the deaf person[4] and something false to the blind person.

(2) The case above involves what are clearly two separate, albeit simultaneous utterances. Now take a case where there's only one utterance. In Sheffield, 'while' means what most English speakers express with 'until'. Imagine that I am speaking to someone from Sheffield and someone from New York at the same time, aware of this difference and aware that each of my audiences thinks theirs is the only English use of the word 'while'. I carefully choose my words and say "It's illegal to drive while drunk". Again, I think the verdict is clear: I've said something false to the Sheffielder and something true to the New Yorker.

(3) Perhaps the closest case to Mental Reservation is one where I am, once more, in a room with a whiteboard addressing a deaf person and a blind person. I write "it is not the case that" and then I say out loud "I am French" at the same time that I write it on the board. Strange as this case is, it again seems right to say that I've said two things:

(A) I've said something true to the deaf person who is reading the whiteboard—*It is not the case that I am French.*

(B) I've said something false to the blind person who cannot see the whiteboard—*I am French.*

The priest, it seems to me then, has said something true to God and something false to his earthly audience. He has done this intentionally, fully knowing the truth values of the relevant claims, and he has knowingly done so in a warranting context. What does our definition of 'lying' say about this?

Lying: If the speaker is not the victim of linguistic error/malapropism or using metaphor, hyperbole, or irony, then they lie iff (1) they say that P; (2) they believe P to be false;[5] (3) they take themself to be in a warranting context.

---

[4] Though the truth of "I am British" might be denied by certain anti-immigrant groups, since I am a naturalized citizen.

[5] Those who think that lies must be false would rephrase this as "they truly believe P to be false".

Because the priest has said two things, this definition gives a mixed verdict about whether or not he has lied.

(A) The priest has lied to his earthly audience. What he said to them was simply *I am not a priest.* Their position is analogous to that of the blind audience in case (3) who cannot see the whiteboard qualification 'it is not the case that': they cannot hear the unspoken qualification 'of Apollo'. What he said to this audience—*I am not a priest*—was false; he knew it to be false; he knew he was in a warranting context; he was speaking literally; and he was not a victim of malapropism or linguistic error.

(B) The priest has spoken truthfully to God. God is able to hear his unspoken qualification, "of Apollo". God's position, then, is like that of the person reading the whiteboard and thus able to perceive the whole utterance. He is able to hear "I am not a Priest of Apollo". This is not a lie, because what is said is true and known by the speaker to be true.[6]

We can, then, make partial sense of the priest's belief that he has avoided lying. Given his beliefs about God, he is reasonable to also believe that he has avoided lying *to God*. But, of course, the priest has lied to his earthly audience. And, indeed, at least some proponents appear to acknowledge that this may be taking place.

We will endeavour to prove that whosoever frameth a true proposition in his mind and uttereth some part thereof in words, which of themselves being taken several from the other part reserved were false, doth not so speak false or lie before God, howsoever he may be thought to lie before men. (Henry Garnet, quoted in Jonsen and Toulmin 1988: 208)

We can now make good sense of both why the priest thought what he was doing was acceptable, and why the vast majority of people thought it was totally unacceptable. To consider the priest's utterance to be perfectly fine, one would need to hold the view that only lies to God matter; if one cares

---

[6] Williams (2002: 104) suggests that it is simply impossible to lie to God so this issue doesn't arise. And this is indeed right, if one understands lying as requiring an intent to deceive: God is meant to be omniscient, and so undeceivable. But if we understand lying as I have suggested in Chapter 1, lying to God *is* possible. One may warrant something even if one knows that it will not be believed because it is known to be false. (Indeed, cases of this sort—those not involving God—were the ones that motivated this understanding.)

about lying to other human beings, the utterance is at the very least problematic. The priests engaging in mental reservation at least *seem* to hold the former—and this is a view that shows deep contempt for others (at least for earthly others).

This, I think, is the reason that most proponents of mental reservation placed some limits of its acceptability. I suspect that even most proponents were ill at ease with the thought that lies to people *don't matter*. So, even if they thought lies to God were the most important, many of them probably also thought that lies to humans should be kept to a minimum. And limitations were often placed on the use of mental reservation. One sort of limitation permitted it only in circumstances where there was an overwhelming need for deception—like avoiding persecution or preserving the confessional seal. In such a situation, a priest attempting to do the right thing would be torn. Lying is wrong, so the priest would not want to lie. But breaking the confessional seal is also wrong. The priest forced to reply, then, would need to find a way to honour both of these thoughts. The doctrine of mental reservation is a way of dealing with this conflict. It functions much like a choice to merely mislead—by giving a way of deceiving which is thought to be slightly better than a garden variety lie. It's still a lie to people, but it's not a lie to God. Since it's still accepted that lying to people is bad, its use is (most plausibly) confined to special circumstances.

Another sort of limitation on the use of mental reservation is also interesting. Domenico Soto argued that only one type of mental reservation was acceptable:

The answer, "I do not know", spoken with the unexpressed qualification, "in a way that I can state publicly"...He was quite certain that it held good in only one type of case: that of a priest asked for information that he knows only from sacramental confession, "for the whole Christian world knows that such information is spoken to the priest as to God". (Jonsen and Toulmin 1988: 199–200)

Here, it seems, what makes the mental reservation acceptable is that it fools nobody. There are two ways this might be interpreted, both interesting:

(1) Since "the whole Christian world" knows that the priest cannot reveal what was said in the confessional, the mental reservation actually is accessible to the audience. On this understanding, the audience knows that the priest must be saying to himself "in such a way as I can state publicly". We can imagine this as analogous to

a case in which elliptical material is so obvious that it counts as part of the sentence uttered (as in the case of syntactic ellipsis, discussed in Chapter 2.) On this reading, the priest has uttered the same sentence to both God and his earthly audience. He has said exactly the same thing to both: that he does not know in such a way that he can state publicly. Since this is true and he knows this, he has not lied to either of them.

(2) Since "the whole Christian world" knows that the priest cannot reveal what was said in the confessional, the lie (to people of course, not God) does not in fact deceive. It is what Sorensen calls a "bald-faced" lie.[7] Sorensen notes that although bald-faced lies are widely condemned, they are in fact arguably much more morally acceptable than other lies:

> The utilitarian explanation of why lying is wrong is that deception has bad consequences. But bald-faced lies are not deceptive. Deontological explanations of why lying is bad turn on the *intent* to deceive . . . But bald-faced lies do not fool anyone . . . Another deontological explanation is that lying involves a betrayal of trust. The liar invites the hearer to take his word for it. But the bald-faced liar has no hope of such treachery. He realizes that his hearer is not going to believe the falsehood. (Sorensen 2007: 252)
>
> All of this applies to the blatant use of mental reservation discussed by Soto. Perhaps an utterance like that which Soto discusses *is* a lie (to people), but as it will very obviously fool nobody, it is a more acceptable lie.

An interesting question is what happens to all of this if we don't accept that God exists and hears the priest's thoughts. A tempting first thought might be that the priest then does not say anything truthful, but only his lie to the earthly audience. However, I think this is wrong. The priest believes that God hears him and he is uttering in a way that he thinks God can hear. Unknown to him, there is nobody who can perceive his utterance. Let's consider an analogy.

I am attempting to use sign language to truthfully say that P to someone I take to be a deaf person who does not read lips. At the same time, I use spoken English to say that not-P to a blind hearing person. However, this time it turns out that the deaf person is actually a very well-constructed cardboard cut-out. Unknown to me, then, nobody perceives my sign language utterance. I don't think this at all undermines the thought that I have said that P.

---

[7] I discuss these in Chapter 1, section 5.

It seems to me that the priest's silent utterance of *I am not a priest of Apollo* in a Godless world is much like my signing at the cardboard cut-out. We have each uttered a sentence that would be perceived by our audience if they existed. The fact that the audience doesn't exist does not affect what we have said.

Regardless of what the proponents of Mental Reservation have said, a further question is still unsettled: how *should we* morally judge the priest who utters (1) due to his adherence to the doctrine of mental reservation? This is trickier, and I suspect views will vary—much as we have seen views to vary in other cases. One possible judgement is that he is genuinely trying to juggle two legitimate goals, keeping the seal of the confessional (or avoiding persecution) and avoiding lying, and that the effort devoted to this reveals something laudable about him. A different judgement would be that only contempt for other humans would allow the priest to so discount the importance of lying to his earthly audience, and that there is nothing praiseworthy about this. Which judgement we make will depend on which virtues we hold to be most important and which facts of the case we focus on. And this seems absolutely right.

The Doctrine of Mental Reservation has recently been invoked in a context where very few of us will find it difficult to come to a verdict about moral acceptability. What follows is a description of a report on investigations into clerical child rape in Dublin.

The report of the independent Commission of Investigation, headed by Judge Yvonne Murphy, said a mental reservation permits a church official knowingly to convey a misleading impression to another person without being guilty of lying.

The report on how allegations of clerical child abuse were handled in the Dublin Archdiocese gave the following example: "John calls (on) the parish priest to make a complaint about the behavior of one of his curates. The parish priest sees him coming but does not want to see him because he considers John to be a trouble-maker. He sends another of his curates to answer the door. John asks the curate if the parish priest is in. The curate replies that he is not. This is clearly untrue but in the church's view it is not a lie, because, when the curate told John that the parish priest was not in, he mentally reserved to himself the words 'to you'", the report said. (Molloy 2009)

The judgement is easy in this case because we don't think, even for a second, that the priest is trying to juggle two noble goals: covering up and thereby facilitating child rape is one of the most reprehensible goals we can imagine. So there is no reason for thinking anything laudable at all is revealed about this priest: we see a contempt both for his interlocutor and for the children of his parish, and nothing more.

2.2 The Doctrine of Equivocation

The Doctrine of Equivocation was a somewhat more widely accepted Casuist doctrine, rather nicely summarized in this quote which Pascal (an opponent) had the Good Father write, in *The Provincial Letters*:

One of the most embarrassing problems is how to avoid lying, especially when one would like people to believe something untrue. This is where our doctrine of equivocation is marvellously helpful, for it allows one "to use ambiguous terms, conveying a different meaning to the hearer from that in which one understands them himself", as Sanchez says, *Moral Works*, II, 3, vi, n. 13.[8]

The doctrine amounts to the careful uttering of an ambiguous phrase, in order to avoid lying. To see how this works, consider some phrase that means both P and Q, where the speaker knows P to be true and Q to be false. The speaker also knows that his audience will take him to have meant Q. Yet, the thought goes, the speaker has not lied because P is true. Although Pascal (and others) opposed this doctrine, it has a bit more going for it than the Doctrine of Mental Reservation, and it has won more support.

One of the nicest examples of an equivocation comes from Raymond of Pennafort (1175–1275). Raymond was discussing Augustine's much-discussed (to this day) case of a person hiding an innocent fugitive in one's house. Augustine held that one could not lie. Raymond suggested that one could legitimately save the innocent fugitive by uttering the Latin sentence "*non est hic*", which carries two meanings:

(3)   he is not here
(3*)   he does not eat here.[9]

(I suppose one would have to make sure that the fugitive eats nothing at one's house.)

[8] Jonsen and Toulmin (1988: 195).
[9] Jonsen and Toulmin (1988: 197).

The Doctrine of Equivocation is a somewhat tricky one to evaluate. Let's review our definition of lying, and consider the "*non est hic*" example.

Lying: If the speaker is not the victim of linguistic error/malapropism or using metaphor, hyperbole, or irony, then they lie iff (1) they say that P; (2) they believe P to be false; (3) they take themself to be in a warranting context.

We know that our speaker is not the victim of linguistic error/malapropism or using metaphor, hyperbole, or irony. So the definition can be applied to his case. Our first question is whether the person (call him 'Raymond') who knows he will be understood as meaning the false (3) counts as lying. Take P to be the content of (3). Raymond knows that P is false, so clause (2) of Lying is satisfied. But what about the other clauses? Clause (3) is really quite easy. Raymond is in a warranting context, and he knows this.

Clause (1) is the tricky one. To satisfy it, Raymond must say that P. Raymond has uttered an ambiguous sentence, which can mean either P or P* (where P* is captured by (3*)). The audience takes him to have said that P. But the view that audience interpretation determines what is said by an ambiguous sentence is very unappealing. Imagine that I am working in a restaurant and I say to my (unknown to me, hungry and cannibalistic co-worker), "The Joneses are ready to eat". Chaos ensues, when all I meant to do was suggest that we should bring them their meals. Surely, despite my co-worker's understanding of my ambiguous utterance I did not say that the Joneses are ready *to be eaten*. If the audience's interpretation could determine what is said by an ambiguous sentence, that would be the case. Far more appealing is the view that the speaker's intention determines what is said. On this view, my desire merely to communicate that we should bring the Joneses their food means that I did not say what my hopeful co-worker thought. But even if we accept that speaker intention makes this determination, things are not straightforward.

One view would have it that *the speaker's meaning* determines what is said: if an ambiguous sentence is uttered, the meaning that the speaker *means* is the one that is said. Speaker meaning, at least as it is usually understood, is a matter of what the speaker intends to convey to the audience. The claim that Raymond intends his audience to grasp is clearly

P. Since this is what Raymond means, on this view it is what he says. Raymond, then, has said that P.

But matters are arguably not quite this simple. If asked, Raymond would (sincerely) deny that he said P. He very much does not intend to *say* that P, even though he intends to convey it. And, arguably, the proposition the speaker *intends to say* is the one that he says with an ambiguous sentence. In normal cases of ambiguity resolution, the speaker intends to say and intends to convey only one of the meanings of the sentence that she utters. What is special about this case is that Raymond intends to say one of the sentence's meanings and to convey the other. And when a speaker's intentions are this fine-grained, there is a good case to be made that what the speaker intends to *say* is what he says. If this is right, then what Raymond says is P* rather than P (even though his audience has no idea of this).

So it's not wholly clear what Raymond has said. It is no surprise, then, that the Doctrine of Equivocation has been viewed as somewhat less clearly reprehensible than the Doctrine of Mental Reservation. My sense is that this also accords fairly well with intuition: while it's difficult to see one who uses Mental Reservation as not doing at least *some* lying, it's far less clear that one who uses Equivocation has lied.

Perhaps because it looks far less clearly like lying than the Doctrine of Mental Reservation, the Doctrine of Equivocation has been viewed as more morally acceptable. We don't, of course, have to agree with this verdict. In fact, our judgements are likely to vary a great deal from case to case, depending on whether we think the Equivocator is nobly trying to steer a path between two morally problematic possibilities, or whether we think he is simply finding an over-clever way to deceive.

2.3 Demonstratives

Alphonsus de Liguori, in his *Summa Sylvestrina*, makes this excellent proposal:

If someone was seeking to kill another person asks you, "did he go this way?" you may answer, "no, not this way," meaning "his feet did not tread the very ground you are pointing at".[10]

---

[10] Jonsen and Toulmin (1988: 198).

This suggestion is particularly interesting for the philosopher of language, since it involves careful exploitation of the fact that even when a demonstrative is combined with a demonstration there may be uncertainty about what, precisely, is being demonstrated. The murderer in the example is meaning to demonstrate a general direction. The protector of the innocent victim (call him 'Alphonsus'), when he utters 'this', claims that he is instead demonstrating a specific bit of ground. Our question now is whether Alphonsus has succeeded in his effort to mislead without lying.

We'll begin by re-displaying our definition of 'lying'.

> Lying: If the speaker is not the victim of linguistic error/malapropism or using metaphor, hyperbole, or irony, then they lie iff (1) they say that P; (2) they believe P to be false;[11] (3) they take themself to be in a warranting context.

Take P to be *no, he did not go*[12] (*understood as in this general direction*). Certainly Alphonsus believes P to be false. It's also clear that Alphonsus is in a warranting context, and that he knows this. Finally, he is speaking literally and not the victim of linguistic error or malapropism. All the clauses except (1), then, are clearly satisfied. The key question is whether he says that P. The answer to this will depend in part on one's views regarding demonstrative reference determination.

On a view like Wettstein's (1984), the referent of a demonstrative will be what is indicated by the cues that a competent audience would take the speaker to be relying on. Interestingly, it will matter a great deal which competent audience one considers. The murderer is presumably a competent audience, and will presumably take the speaker to be indicating the general direction (which is what he took his own gesture to indicate). This suggests that the referent will be the general direction, and that P will therefore be said. But imagine now another competent audience, who is a well-trained Jesuit follower of Alphonsus. Imagine even that Alphonsus takes his remark to be addressed to both of these (so that both are his audience). This competent audience will know what Alphonsus is up to, and he will take him to be indicating a specific bit of ground. If this

---

[11] Those who think that lies must be false would rephrase this as "they truly believe P to be false".

[12] I'm taking syntactic ellipsis to be responsible for the fact that *he* and *go* make it into P.

competent audience is the one that matters, Alphonsus has not said that P. Wettstein's view, then, leaves us somewhat uncertain about what has been said.

An alternative view (that of Kaplan 1989a) would be that the demonstrative gesture alone determines the reference. This view has some appeal when we consider cases where a person uses a demonstrative gesture, accompanied by a pointing, without realizing what she is pointing to. (Think of the person who thinks she is pointing at a picture of Carnap when she accidentally points at a picture of George W. Bush and says "that is a picture of a brilliant man".)[13] But it is less appealing when we turn to cases like the current one, where the question is exactly *how specific* a thing is picked out by a pointing gesture (a general direction or a patch of ground). Colin McGinn suggests that the referent of 'that F' will be "the first F to intersect the line projected from the speaker's pointing finger" (Braun 2008). So the way that is referred to, on this view, is the first way to intersect the line projected from Alphonsus's pointing finger. Presumably, this means that the bit of ground indicated is indeed the referent, and that Alphonsus has not lied.[14] But this view really isn't a very appealing one. To see this, imagine instead that Alphonsus wanted to be helpful to the murderer, so readily told him "yes, he went this way". On McGinn's view, Alphonsus would thereby have uttered an accidental falsehood, since he didn't pass over that very bit of ground.

Next, consider a view on which the speaker's intention determines the referent of her pointing gesture. For Bach (1992), the referent of a demonstrative is determined by the speaker's referential intention:[15]

a referential intention isn't just any intention to refer to something one has in mind but is the intention that one's audience identify, and take themself to be intended to identify, a certain item as the referent by means of thinking of it a certain identifiable way . . . Such an intention is goes unfulfilled if the audience fails to identify the right individual in the right way, that is, the one intended in the way intended. (Bach 1992: 143)

---

[13] I'm updating Kaplan's famous example.

[14] Of course, ways are rather odd objects, so it's possible to argue over this.

[15] It's worth recalling that Bach now doesn't think this referent makes it into what is said (although he did when he wrote his 1992 paper). But on the view of saying needed for the lying–misleading distinction, demonstrative referents do make it into what is said. (For more discussion, see Chapters 2 and 3.)

On Bach's view, then, a referential intention is (roughly) an intention that one's audience identify the referent by means of thinking of it in the right way. So the only object that can be the referent determine by this sort of intention will be an object that the speaker intends the audience to identify. And the object Alphonsus intends his audience to identify is the general direction, *not* the specific bit of ground. If we employ Bach (1992)'s view on demonstrative reference, then, Alphonsus *has* said that P—that he did not go in this general direction. He has said something he knows to be false. And he has lied.

An alternative version of the speaker intention view is that the referent of a demonstrative is whatever object the speaker has in mind and intends as the referent of her demonstrative. (This is the view that Kaplan 1989b seems to hold.) On this view, as long as Alphonsus intends the patch of ground as the demonstrative's reference, it is. So Alphonsus succeeds in saying the truth that he did not pass over this particular piece of grass, and does not say the falsehood, P. But this is not a wildly appealing view, as Marga Reimer (1991a, b) has convincingly argued. It would mean that I say something true if, thinking it to be of Carnap, I accidentally point at the picture of Bush, and say "that is a picture of a brilliant man". It would mean that I can never speak falsely when I point and say "those are my keys", as long as I *think* I am pointing at my keys (an example from Reimer).

So does Alphonsus's careful use of demonstratives succeed in allowing him to avoid saying the false claim that he wants to convey? We can't answer this question until we settle some difficult questions about demonstrative reference. But our uncertainty accords, I think, with intuitions about the example: it really is a tough case.

And, importantly, we need not agree with Alphonsus's own view that what he has done is morally superior to lying. As we have seen, whether or not some claim is a lie rather than some other sort of deception does not on its own have any effect on its moral status. Our moral judgement of Alphonsus's deception is likely to depend on whether we think it is good that he cares so much about lying that he has carefully exploited demonstratives to avoid it—or whether we think one who cares so much about lying in this situation clearly has the wrong priorities. (This is perfectly parallel to our likely thoughts about the more traditional murderer at the door case, which we've already discussed in Chapter 4.)

3 Completion cases

Completion cases were very tricky for our theory of what is said. So it's worth revisiting them here, to see what happens when we consider not just what is said, but also our ethical evaluations of what is taking place. We'll begin with a return to our various versions of the murderous nurse example, which was very important in Chapters 2 and 3. In this example, Dave is lying in a hospital bed, and two nurses are discussing the treatment he needs. Ed holds up a bottle of heart medicine, points at it, and utters (4):

(4)   Has Dave had enough?

Fred replies with (5):

(5)   Dave's had enough.

As it turns out, Fred hates Dave, wants him to die, and plans to bring this about by denying him his much-needed heart medicine. When he uttered (5), Fred meant something like (5*), (5**), or (5***), which he knew to be false.

(5*)   Dave's had enough heart medicine.
(5**)   Dave's had enough of that.
(5***)   Dave's had enough of the stuff in that bottle you're holding up.

As we saw in Chapter 3, there are some tricky technical issues about how exactly to handle the uncertainty over what is said by this utterance. But, whichever method we choose, it is clear that Fred has lied. And we have no difficulty with our moral assessment of the situation. Fred has deliberately lied in order to kill Dave. Judging this to be wrong is totally straightforward.

But in Chapter 3 we also saw some slightly trickier cases. In one such case, non-murderous Gertrude wrongly takes Ed to be holding up a whisky bottle, and rightly wants to indicate that Dave's had enough whisky. So she utters (5).

(5)   Dave's had enough.

Unfortunately, Ed was holding up a bottle of Dave's much-needed heart medicine. As we saw in Chapter 3, Gertrude has clearly not lied. Our uncertainty about whether she said something about whisky makes no difference to our judgement about whether she's lied, then. It also makes no difference to our moral judgement—nothing hinges, morally, on whether someone has said something true or accidentally said something false.

The tougher case is that of murderous Fred walking in on non-murderous Ed, about to give Dave a cup of tea. Wrongly taking Ed to be about to give Dave his heart medicine, Fred intervenes by uttering (5):

(5)   Dave's had enough.

Intuitively, we're really not sure whether Fred has said that Dave's had enough heart medicine, and so we're not sure whether he's lied.[16] But this uncertainty does not lead to any moral uncertainty. And now we can make sense of this. Whether or not someone has *lied* is not in itself morally significant. Sometimes, the choice between lying and merely intentionally misleading can be morally revealing about a person's character. But there is no such revealing element of choice here. Fred has attempted to deceive Ed by lying in order to bring about Dave's death. Luckily for Dave, he has failed to deceive Ed because Ed does not understand Fred's utterance in the way that it was intended. But whether this failed deception attempt included an actual lie or not is totally uninteresting from a moral point of view. It reveals nothing whatsoever of moral significance. It is not so surprising, then, that our intuitions about saying are a bit unclear when we come to cases like this: we simply don't need a notion of saying which gives clear verdicts for this sort of case.

4 The Empire State Building, and jumping elsewhere

Consider once more sentence (6), which we discussed quite a bit in Chapter 2.

(6)   Billy went to the top of the Empire State Building and jumped.

According to the view suggested here, what is said by an utterance of (6) does not include anything about what sort of jumping took place

---

[16] If Fred has said that Dave's had enough tea, it doesn't seem that he's lied: Fred doesn't have any opinion whatsoever about whether Dave has had enough tea. If Fred has failed to say anything truth evaluable he hasn't lied, for familiar reasons. So the only way that he's lied is if he's said that Dave's had enough heart medicine (or something like this).

(since this would be a matter of Expansion not Completion). Nor does it include anything about the sequence of events. The cases we discussed in the previous chapter led us to believe that this sort of conception was desirable. But it may start to look problematic once we reflect that an utterance of (6) might be made true by a scenario on which Billy jumps on the bed when he is five years old, and then twenty years later takes the lift to the top of the Empire State Building and back down again.

I think this point *looks* problematic, but that once we think more carefully about lying and misleading, it turns out not to be. Recall again our final definition of 'lying'.

> Lying: If the speaker is not the victim of linguistic error/malapropism or using metaphor, hyperbole, or irony, then they lie iff (1) they say that P; (2) they believe P to be false;[17] (3) they take themself to be in a warranting context.

Now, imagine that Lou wants to upset Pablo by making Pablo believe that Billy has jumped off the top of the Empire State Building (which Lou knows to be untrue). Lou utters (6), with the intention of lying to Pablo:

(6)   Billy went to the top of the Empire State Building and jumped.

As it turns out, however, Billy did once jump on his bed and he did once go to the top of the Empire State Building. On the view put forward here, that means that Lou's utterance of (6) says something true. But Lou believes it to be false. So, on the definition above, clauses (1) and (2) are satisfied. Lou knows it's a warranting context, he's speaking literally, and he is not the victim of malapropism or linguistic error. Lou's utterance, then, is clearly a lie.[18]

---

[17] Those who think that lies must be false would rephrase this as "they truly believe P to be false".

[18] In this case, it makes a very big difference that we have chosen to allow for the possibility of lying by saying something true which one believes to be false. If we required (as some do) that what is said must in fact be false, Lou's utterance is not a lie. I think this is a less intuitive result than the one that we get with the definition I have defended. However, those whose intuitions rule out true lies will probably find it preferable. Morally speaking, nothing will turn on this. This is because, morally speaking, nothing at all turns simply on whether a case is one of lying or misleading. What matters morally is what has been revealed about the speaker's moral character, and whether we accept the 'knows' or 'believes' version of clause (2) reveals nothing whatsoever about Lou's moral character. From Lou's perspective, nothing turns on this decision. Lou takes himself to be lying, no matter what we decide about this. And this seems right. A view on which the lying–misleading distinction is, in and of itself, of

It seems to me this is a perfectly reasonable result for this case. If we explained to Lou that actually he'd said something true, I think he would accept this—though he would rightly take this to be not very interesting or relevant. The sense that there was a problem here, it seems to me, comes from the fact that Lou was thinking about Billy jumping off the Empire State Building; this is what he was trying to communicate; and this is what Pablo presumably took Lou to be communicating. But, importantly, none of this means that it was what Lou said—in the sense that matters for lying and misleading.

Now consider a slightly different case, that of a more devious speaker than Lou—call her Louisa. Louisa wants to avoid lying to Pablo (she's a Kantian, at least about that), but she too wants him to believe that Billy jumped off the top of the Empire State Building. Her sole reason for this is to cause Pablo distress.[19] Louisa reflects carefully, and realizes that she could say something true by uttering (6), while still misleading Pablo. Does she thereby succeed in avoiding lying? Our answer must be yes, for she knows that she is saying something true—she does not take herself to be saying something false. Clause (2) of Lying fails to be satisfied.

What sort of moral judgement should we make about Louisa? Well, this will vary. Perhaps we will take seriously Louisa's effort to mitigate the wrong she is doing, and see her as struggling defensibly to find a means of deceiving other than lying. In that case, we may judge her a little less harshly than if she had outright lied. More likely, though, we will not see anything at all defensible about what Louisa is doing. We'll think that if she was (rightly) uncomfortable with her deception she should not have deceived at all. After all, there was no *good* reason for her deception: she did it only to upset Pablo. We may in fact judge her more harshly for her careful choice of words—thinking that it functions mainly as a way for her to avoid facing up to the wrong that she is doing.

5 Clinton's utterances, and perjury

President Bill Clinton's testimony regarding his relationship with Monica Lewinsky is by far the most-discussed recent case in which the lying–

---

moral significance would seem to wrongly attribute moral significance to a judgement like this.

[19] Assume also that she has no good justification for this desire.

misleading distinction looms large. And it is a very intricate and interesting case to examine, both philosophically and politically. Many of the common beliefs about it are not right, and there are quite a lot of intriguing complexities. I'll be focused here on the perjury charges against Clinton, as they were the basis of his impeachment, and so particularly important. It is perhaps worth warning the reader that this discussion will be a lengthy one. I think the length is merited by both the philosophical interest and the real-world importance of the case.

A bit of background is called for. According to Paula Jones, Clinton sexually harassed her when he was Governor of Arkansas. She filed a lawsuit, *Clinton* v. *Jones*, while he was President. While President, Clinton also had a consensual affair with Monica Lewinsky. Through a complicated chain of events, Paula Jones's lawyers learned of this affair and asked Clinton about it in his deposition for the *Jones* trial. Perjury charges for this deposition were brought against Clinton before a federal grand jury. The judge in the *Jones* trial eventually ruled that Clinton's testimony regarding Lewinsky was inadmissible because irrelevant—everyone agreed that the Lewinsky affair was consensual, so it had no bearing on a sexual harassment case. Under US law, the *Jones* deposition could not then count as perjurious, even if Clinton had knowingly lied. The deposition given to the grand jury regarding possible perjury charges, however, could count as perjury. *This* deposition provided the basis for Clinton's impeachment, on the charge that he lied to the Grand Jury. (The House rejected impeachment charges which were based on a charge of perjury during the *Jones* deposition.)[20]

There are four particular utterances we will examine (along with some variants), in the four following sections.

5.1 The meaning of 'is'

Elsewhere in this book, I have discussed *Clinton's* utterance of the sentence "there is no improper relationship" in an interview. This utterance had nothing whatsoever to do with the perjury case, nor did any similar present-tensed utterance by *Clinton*. The utterance which led to much journalistic and political mockery about Clinton discussing what the meaning of 'is' is, was actually one by Clinton's lawyer, Robert Bennett.

---

[20] See Solan and Tiersma (2005: 222–3).

During the *Clinton* v. *Jones* deposition, Bennett objected to questions being asked, by making the following utterance:

I question the good faith of counsel, the innuendo of the question. Counsel is fully aware that Ms Lewinsky has filed—has an affidavit, which they are in possession of, saying that there is absolutely no sex of any kind in any manner, shape or form with President Clinton.[21]

During the grand jury proceedings, prosecutors accused Clinton of perjury because he did not correct this utterance. They claimed that he made:

an "utterly false statement" by not speaking up and correcting his lawyer's comment. Clinton rejoined that Bennett's statement was not necessarily false: "It depends on what the meaning of the word 'is' is".[22]

This utterance by Clinton was widely mocked, and criticized as showing Clinton's slippery, duplicitous nature. There are a few things we should note. First, Clinton is absolutely right that the truth of Bennett's statement depends on the meaning of the word 'is'.[23] Moreover, he's right that Bennett's statement is literally true: it is utterly uncontentious that Clinton and Lewinsky were not having sex at the time of Bennett's utterance.[24] Even if Clinton had said "What Bennett just said is true", he would not have been lying. However, the prosecutors' claim was that Clinton had lied and thereby committed perjury by *not saying anything*. This is quite clearly wrong, as a matter of ordinary language, and as a matter of law, and according to our definition of lying. In order to lie, one must say *something*. And, except in very special cases (of which this was not one),[25] it is not possible to commit perjury without saying something.

It's clear, then, that Clinton did not commit perjury by failing to correct his lawyer's literally true statement. (In fact, he couldn't have committed perjury in the *Jones* trial, the one at issue here, since his testimony was ruled

---

[21] Bennett, quoted in Solan and Tiersma (2005: 229).

[22] Solan and Tiersma (2005: 229).

[23] And also, of course, on the meanings of other words.

[24] It's obviously and uninterestingly true if we read 'there is no sex . . . with President Clinton' in its most limited literal sense: Clinton may have been a risk-taker with regard to his sex life, but he would not have had sex with Lewinsky in the deposition room, in the presence of Jones's lawyers. But it was also true construed a bit more broadly: the sexual relationship was over by the time of the Jones trial.

[25] Solan and Tiersma (2005: 230). The only instance in which one might be vulnerable to perjury charges without speaking would be very special cases in which there was some legal obligation to speak up, of which this was not one.

inadmissible.) It's also clear that he did not lie in this instance, and that he didn't even make a misleading utterance.

5.2 Sexual relations, as discussed by Clinton

During the *Jones* deposition, Clinton was asked if he had had sexual relations with Lewinsky and he denied that he had done so. This was a part of the basis for the grand jury perjury charge, since clearly something sexual did go on between Clinton and Lewinsky. It's widely believed that Clinton lied in denying sexual relations with Lewinsky at the *Jones* deposition. But in this deposition a very specific definition of 'sexual relations' had been agreed to, and it was a rather unusual one:

A person engages in 'sexual relations' when the person knowingly engages in or causes contact with the genitalia, anus, groin, breast, inner thigh, or buttocks of any person with an intent to arouse or gratify the sexual desire of any person.[26]

5.2.1 The definition's standard interpretation Legal experts on language (e.g. Solan and Tiersma (2005); Green (2006)) seem agreed that having oral sex performed on one would not count as engaging in sexual relations under this definition, though being the performer of the oral sex would. In this section, we will assume this understanding to be correct. Clinton claims that, although Lewinsky performed oral sex on him, he never engaged in any contact with any of the listed areas of her body. If that is true[27] (I call this the 'Selfish Lover Defence'),[28] then Clinton's denial of sexual relations at the *Jones* trial was true, and he knew it to be true. It was very clearly not perjury (which it couldn't have been in any case, since it was ruled inadmissible). Moreover, it was not a lie under our definition of 'lie'. It was, however, extremely misleading.

So what moral judgement should we make regarding it? Well, a first thought is simply to look, as I've suggested we should in general do, at what the choice to mislead rather than lie reveals about Clinton. The conclusion we reach this way will be highly dependent on our views about other factors. One who thinks Clinton was being unfairly

---

[26] Green (2006: 142).

[27] Like many others, I find it very difficult to believe that this is true, and it certainly conflicts with Lewinsky's testimony, but let's assume it for the sake of discussion. Otherwise, Clinton's utterance was just a lie, and not terribly interesting to discuss.

[28] Another form of Selfish Lover Defence has it that Clinton did touch these parts of Lewinsky's body, but not with the intent of arousing or gratifying her. I call this the Even More Selfish Lover Defence.

persecuted and pursued for a consensual affair that was not the court's business may be very tolerant of his effort to be truthful while at the same time not revealing such private matters. Clinton himself later maintained that this was what he was doing, accepting that it was his responsibility to answer questions truthfully, but that "it was not my responsibility, in the face of their repeated illegal leaking, it was not my responsibility to volunteer a lot of information" (Solan and Tiersma 2005: 224). One who thinks that the court and the public had every right to know about the Lewinsky affair will take Clinton to have used underhanded means to avoid his moral responsibility to offer this information. But I think we can get beyond this partisan stalemate when we recall that we are concerned with a denial in a courtroom, which both Clinton and all the other lawyers and judges present knew to be governed by the perjury rules we have already discussed, according to which one's obligation is only to say what is literally true. With this restricted conception of a speaker's responsibility in place, there was plausibly no moral obligation for Clinton to avoid misleading—the obligation to prevent misleading utterances fell squarely and explicitly on the shoulders of the lawyers questioning him, who could and should have insisted on a different definition of 'sexual relations'.

5.2.2 Revisiting the definition As I have noted, there is substantial legal agreement that the definition above is narrow enough that having oral sex performed on one does not count as sexual relations. But I'm not actually thoroughly convinced by this. In fact, it seems to me that the definition, as written, is extremely broad.

A person engages in 'sexual relations' when the person knowingly engages in or causes contact with the genitalia, anus, groin, breast, inner thigh, or buttocks of any person with an intent to arouse or gratify the sexual desire of any person.

If we take Clinton to be the referent of 'a person' and to satisfy both instances of 'any person', I would think that the contact he has admitted to counts as engaging in sexual relations. After all, Clinton did cause contact with the genitalia of some person—himself—in order to arouse or gratify the sexual desire of some person—also himself. The only way to deny this would be to assign Clinton no causal role in the oral sex event, which seems highly unlikely given the power dynamics between President and intern.

It's worth noting, however, *just how broad* the definition is on my interpretation. Suppose that two of my friends have been whingeing about their non-existent sex lives. I introduce them to each other, hoping that this will solve the problem. It does, and they have sexual relations involving contact with all of the listed body parts. I have thereby caused contact with the listed body parts, and done so with the intent of causing sexual gratification (for my friends). So, by making this introduction, I have engaged in sexual relations. This seems to me excessively broad.

Suppose now that I am right: the definition is extremely (indeed excessively) broad, and does cover being the recipient of oral sex. But suppose also that the Selfish Lover Defence was true (Clinton never touched any of Lewinsky's listed body parts), and that Clinton genuinely understood the definition in the narrower way suggested by commentators. If that's right, then Clinton said something false without realizing it, because he was wrong about the meaning of a word that he used. We already know that Clinton didn't thereby commit perjury, since his utterance was ruled inadmissible. But it would not have been perjury in any case, because he didn't know it to be false. Nor would he have lied, according to our definition. In fact, this case would be one on which our definition failed to give a verdict, as it would be one of linguistic error.

> Lying: If the speaker is not the victim of linguistic error/malapropism or using metaphor, hyperbole, or irony, then they lie iff (1) they say that P; (2) they believe P to be false; (3) they take themself to be in a warranting context.[29]

What Clinton said, on the current hypothesis, was false. It was the claim that he did not engage in sexual relations with Lewinsky, on the broad interpretation of the definition. What's more, he knew this claim to be false. Clauses (1) and (2) are thus satisfied. Moreover, clause (3) is satisfied: he knew himself to be in a warranting context, and he was speaking literally. However, the case is not one of lying because Clinton, wrong about the meaning of 'sexual relations', was a victim of linguistic error. Although he said something false, he did not realize this was what he was saying: *he accidentally said something false.* This variant of the Clinton case turns out to be a great deal like the rock climber Anna, unwittingly saying

---

[29] One who believes that lies must be false would add that P must be false.

in Spanish that many English people climb without clothes (from Chapter 1, section 7.2).

5.2.3 Outside the Jones *trial* Clinton also sometimes denied having had sexual relations with Lewinsky on occasions outside the *Jones* trial. On these occasions, he insisted, he was using a definition of 'sexual relations' such that only penetrative genital to genital intercourse counts as sexual relations. Lewinsky also denied having had sexual relations with Clinton in an affidavit to the *Jones* case, which was not governed by any stipulated legal definition of 'sexual relations'. Clinton testified during the *Jones* proceedings that what she said was true, and he was questioned about this at the grand jury hearing. He defended the truth of her statement by suggesting that she was using a definition of 'sexual relations' on which only penetrative genital to genital intercourse would count as sex, and that this was also the definition that "most ordinary Americans" would probably give (Solan and Tiersma 2005: 223).

As a matter of fact, Clinton was probably right about most ordinary Americans, according to Sanders and Reinisch (1999), who found that 59 per cent would not consider oral–genital conduct to be sex.[30] It's also clear that Lewinsky herself adhered to such a definition, as she made very clear during the phone conversations that Linda Tripp recorded without her knowledge ('Tripp–Lewinsky Tapes 7', CBS News 1998). Bearing this in mind, it seems clear that neither Clinton nor Lewinsky was lying in denying sexual relations: the definition they used was the one commonly used in their linguistic community (assuming that community to be "ordinary Americans", and assuming that Sanders and Reinisch's results accurately represent the views of ordinary Americans); and it was also, if we believe them on this, their own intended definition. If this is right, then what they thought they said in denying sexual relations was not falsified by having had oral sex. It was, then, true. Moreover, they knew it to be true, so they could not have been lying by saying it. And, if they genuinely thought that most people used this definition, they *may* even not have been trying to mislead (with these utterances).

It's interesting to consider, however, what would have been the case if Clinton had been wrong about "ordinary Americans". Suppose that the

---

[30] Unsurprisingly, views are very different with a sample of just gay, lesbian, and bisexual Americans, with 88–89 per cent counting oral–genital contact as sex (Mustanski 2001).

overwhelming majority of ordinary Americans in fact did take oral sex to count as sex. But suppose that Clinton and Lewinsky were in fact using the term to refer only to penetrative genital to genital sex, due to their mistaken belief that this was the meaning of 'sex'. What would we say about this case? This case is another one of linguistic error, again analogous to the rock climber accidentally saying in Spanish that many British people climb without clothes. Clinton and Lewinsky would have accidentally said something false. But, due to their linguistic error, our definition would not give a verdict on whether or not they lied.

> Lying: If the speaker is not the victim of linguistic error/malapropism or using metaphor, hyperbole, or irony, then they lie iff (1) they say that P; (2) they believe P to be false;[31] (3) they take themself to be in a warranting context.

5.3 Times alone

The final allegation of Clinton lies that we'll consider is the one that has received the least attention, though it is arguably the most compelling case for an accusation of lying. During the Jones deposition, Clinton was repeatedly asked whether he was alone with Monica Lewinsky in the Oval Office. Here's one response:

Passage A: I don't recall . . . She—it seems to me she brought things to me once or twice on the weekends. In that case, whatever time she would be in there, drop it off, exchange a few words and go, she was there.[32]

The prosecutor followed up, and Clinton replied, as below.

Passage B: Q. So I understand, your testimony is that it was possible, then, that you were alone with her, but you have no specific recollection of that ever happening?

A. Yes, that's correct. It's possible that she, in, while she was working there, brought something to me and that at the time she brought it to me, she was the only person there. That's possible.[33]

In each of these answers from Clinton, there are two parts. First, there is a claim that he doesn't remember whether he was alone with Lewinsky

---

[31] Those who think that lies must be false would rephrase this as "they truly believe P to be false".

[32] Solan and Tiersma (2005: 225).

[33] Solan and Tiersma (2005: 226).

(or that he lacks a specific recollection). These claims of memory loss are almost certain to be false, and to have been known by Clinton to be false. Clinton said them, they were (almost certainly) false, and he knowingly warranted their truth. He was speaking literally, and not the victim of linguistic error or malapropism. They were, then, lies. (And if they'd been admissible, they would have been perjury.)

The second parts of the Clinton utterances are more careful. Look at Passage A first. It is probably true that Lewinsky sometimes brought him things on the weekends and was briefly alone with him. This makes the claim true. Clinton's utterance also *suggests* that these were the only times Lewinsky was alone with him. But he does not say this. Instead, he carefully crafted a misleading statement. The prosecutor could have followed up by asking if those were the only times that Clinton and Lewinsky might have been alone, but he did not do so.

The situation is similar with the second part of Passage B. It is *of course* possible that Clinton and Lewinsky might have been alone when she brought something to him—it happened, after all. Once more, Clinton suggests but does not say that these were the only times they might have been alone. And once more, the prosecutor could and should have followed up with more specific questioning.

If it had not been for the claims of lack of memory, Clinton's above utterances would have been misleading but not lies.[34] In part, our moral evaluation of them will (as I've already noted) depend on what we take them to reveal about his character, which will depend on other beliefs of ours.

6 The Malagasy

The Malagasy of Madagascar seem at first to be a group who place a very strong emphasis on the lying–misleading distinction, regularly doing the latter but not the former. According to Elinor (Ochs) Keenan (1977), conversational norms are somewhat different in this group.[35] They live in close-knit communities in which almost all information is common knowledge. Possessing information that others don't have is a rare and powerful

---

[34] I'm following Solan and Tiersma in this conclusion.

[35] She argues that Grice's conversational maxims don't apply, but this claim will not be our focus here.

position to be in. As a result, people are reluctant to part with such information. Among the Malagasy, it would be perfectly normal to respond to (7) with (8), even if one knows where one's mother is.

(7)   Where is your mother?
(8)   She's either in the kitchen or the garden.

However, Keenan does not give any indication that outright lying—saying something false—is in any way acceptable among the Malagasy. It might seem, then, that misleading is perfectly acceptable while lying is not.

However, this would be a mistaken judgement. For a British person, (7) would be a misleading response, leading the questioner to believe that the answerer is unaware of his mother's location. But for the Malagasy, no misleading takes place—only evasiveness. Because this evasiveness is *expected*, the Malagasy questioner would not in fact assume that the answerer does not know where his mother is. There is, then, no reason to suppose that the Malagasy take misleading to be acceptable.

7 Tact and politeness

Tact often demands that one *not say* certain things, and circumstances can make this very difficult to do. Considerations of tact lead to a range of cases of misleading that are often judged to be acceptable.

Adler (1997: 447) offers the case of Larry, in a social setting, asking Mark, "where's Laura?" (where Laura is Mark's wife). Mark, who has just separated from Laura, replies truthfully "she is away on business". Adler notes that Mark has thereby misled Larry into believing that everything is fine, but that we judge this to be morally acceptable. This, then, gives us a case of polite misleading. Brown and Levinson's cross-cultural study, *Politeness* (1987), documents many further instances of what they call 'indirection' (132) or 'going off record' (211). Many of these are cases of misleading without lying. As they note, this is an important strategy cross-culturally for 'saving face'—that is, avoiding embarrassment to oneself or others.

As I argued in Chapter 4, what really matters to us most is what a particular act of misleading or lying reveals about a person. One who has chosen to mislead out of tact or politeness is one who is trying to avoid saying something problematic, while at the same time trying not to lie. The act they choose, misleading, actually has the same moral status as the act of lying on my view. But if their motivation for choosing it is a good one, we are likely to approve (or at least to not judge it so harshly).

Interestingly, as Brown and Levinson note, there are also polite bald-faced lies—cases in which someone says something so obviously false that there is no chance of being believed. Among the Tzeltal Maya, for example, it is considered perfectly acceptable respond to a request with an obviously false reason for not being able to comply (Brown and Levinson (1987: 116)). This is because refusing the request without such a reason would be offensive. And this is not actually so exotic as it seems. Suppose that I have been served a disastrous dinner by some friends: most of the food was burnt beyond recognition, the rest was boiled into mush, and the hosts forgot to put any spices in. It is obvious to everyone, including the hosts, that the food was terrible. Nonetheless, at the end of the evening, I say, "The food was lovely!" This, arguably, is a polite bald-faced lie. This sort of lie is generally not judged harshly due to its kindly motivation.

But in some cases, due to the role of convention in politeness, there may be room for argument about whether an apparent polite bald-faced lie really is a lie. Begin with the Tzeltal Maya. The Tzeltal also have a special tone of voice that can be used in polite or formal exchanges, "which operates as a kind of giant hedge on everything that is said . . . releasing the speaker from responsibility for believing the truth of what he utters" (Brown and Levinson (1987: 173)). At first glance, this seems like a special case of the tactful bald-faced lie. But this may not in fact be the right treatment. After all, in order to lie a speaker must believe themself to be warranting the truth of what they say, and a tone of voice which releases "the speaker from responsibility for believing the truth of what he utters" sounds as though it is a conventional way of *not warranting* what one is saying. Similarly, one might argue that praising the food at a dinner party is so conventional, and so demanded by etiquette, that the context is not a warranting one.

Some even more complex cases relating to politeness occur for speakers of Egyptian Arabic. David Wilmsen notes that Egyptian Arabic speakers often find themselves in conversational situations in which they "wish to engage in conversation, or indeed feel compelled to do so, while at the same time concealing the truth" (2009: 255). I'll discuss two such situations of special interest to us here. First is the case of responses to inquiries about one's health. It is very common to use the euphemism "tired" to refer to serious ill health. But, of course, "tired" is also used when one actually is just a bit tired. Assuming that the euphemistic use should be treated as an idiom, this means that the term is ambiguous. Suppose, then, that you are a very unhealthy speaker of Egyptian Arabic. Someone inquires after your health, and you want to conceal your illness. You choose to say, "I'm tired". You'd really like your audience to think that you're simply tired and not ill. But the utterance you've chosen—the standard one for this purpose—is an ambiguous one. Have you lied? Whether or not you've lied will turn on whether you've said that you're tired (as in suffering just from fatigue). Call this claim T. If you have said that T, then you've lied, since you know that T is false, you know yourself to be in a warranting context, you aren't speaking non-literally, and you're not a victim of linguistic error or malapropism. But it's genuinely unclear whether you've said that T—you've chosen an ambiguous term, hoping that you'll be taken to be saying that T but not knowing whether you will be. It may be that this is part of the point of the custom—the murkiness about whether or not one is lying helps to make the potential deception seem more acceptable. But it also seems likely that lies of this sort are considered morally unproblematic, since they are so standard, and since it seems very reasonable to want to conceal something so personal as one's ill health.

According to Wilmsen, speakers of Egyptian Arabic will also often refer to people with the wrong names or pronouns of the wrong gender to avoid envy, disapproval or bad luck. Sometimes a speaker will use a false name when talking to someone who is not aware that the name is false. They might, for example, say "Noor is coming" when they mean that Ali is coming, speaking to someone who doesn't realize that Noor is a false name. Again, it's not entirely clear whether or not this is a lie. Much as in the demonstrative cases discussed earlier, it's a bit unclear what is said. Does 'Noor' refer to to Ali, who the speaker has in mind? It might be able to do this, if we treat it as another name for Ali. (If we don't, then it could at best be a case of speaker-reference to Ali, but even that is unclear.) Or does 'Noor' refer to Noor, who the audience will take to be the referent (just as the speaker expects them to)? If 'Noor' refers to Noor, then the speaker has lied. But if 'Noor' refers to Ali, then the speaker hasn't lied—though they have misled. 'Noor' might also fail to refer, again making lying impossible. This sort of utterance is apparently quite standard, and widely accepted. Again, the unclarity about reference may be comforting to the speaker who wants to avoid lying. But more likely this issue simply doesn't matter—since it is a practice that is accepted and expected. Even more complex cases may occur when one uses a false name in talking to someone who knows that the name is false, while being overheard by one who does not. In such a case, depending on what we decide about what is said, one seems to be lying to or misleading one audience, while being wholly truthful to another.

One's professional position may also require one to be tactful, sometimes in a misleading way. In January 2010, David Miliband was thought to have been involved in an attempt to oust Gordon Brown as leader of the Labour Party in the UK. When the attempt failed, and Miliband (one of Brown's cabinet) was asked for comment, he responded with, "I am working closely with the prime minister on foreign policy issues and support the re-election campaign for a Labour government that he is leading" (Wintour *et al.* (2010)). Miliband, as a cabinet member, needed to say something that could be interpreted as an expression of support for Brown. But it seems very clear that Miliband didn't actually support *Brown*. So he made an utterance which he hoped would mislead people into thinking that he did, while at the same time avoiding a lie. I doubt very much, however, if Miliband's utterance succeeded in misleading anyone at all—it was very clearly simply what his position required, and very clearly not a real endorsement. It was what we might call a "bald-faced-misleading-attempt".[36] On the view I developed in Chapter 4, the fact that Miliband attempted to mislead does not make his act a better one than it would have been if it was a lie. And this, I think, feels right.

8 Exploitation of mishearing

As Roy Sorensen notes in his 2011 'What Lies behind Misspeaking', a speaker may also exploit the fact that they are likely to be misheard. Consider, for example, a speaker who says "of course the coffee is free trade", intending to be misheard as having said that the coffee is fair trade. At first this seems like quite a tricky case, but it actually turns out not to be. Clearly, the speaker has not *said* that the coffee is fair trade—so they have not lied. (We know this, because 'free trade' simply does not mean fair trade.)[37] It's also quite clear that they've said that of course the coffee is free trade, even though they expect that they won't be

---

[36] Though we probably shouldn't, as it's a hideous phrase.
[37] Sorensen agrees with this verdict.

properly understood. Instead, the speaker is carefully misleading—though doing so via a somewhat unusual method. On the view I've put forward, this act of merely misleading is not morally preferable to a corresponding act of lying. However, depending on what it reveals it might affect our moral assessment of the speaker.

9 Out-of-context quotation

In the summer of 2010, the United States was briefly consumed by a scandal that turned out to arise from an out-of-context quotation. Shirley Sherrod was Georgia State Director of Rural Development for the Department of Agriculture (not a post that usually attracts much national attention). She became nationally notorious when Andrew Breitbart, a right-wing blogger, quoted her and posted a video of her uttering the following:

> You know, the first time I was faced with helping a white farmer save his farm, he took a long time talking but he was trying to show me he was superior to me. I know what he was doing. But he had come to me for help. What he didn't know, while he was taking all that time trying to show me he was superior to me, was I was trying to decide just how much help I was going to give him. I was struggling with the fact that so many black people had lost their farmland. And here I was faced with having to help a white person save their land. So, I didn't give him the full force of what I could do. I did enough so that when he . . . I assumed the Department of Agriculture had sent him to me, either that, or the Georgia Department of Agriculture, and he needed to go back and report that I did try to help him. So I took him to a white lawyer that had attended some of the training that we had provided because Chapter 12 bankruptcy had just been enacted for the family farm. So I figured if I take him to one of them, that his own kind would take care of him. That's when it was revealed to me that it's about poor versus those who have, and not so much about white – it *is* about white and black, but it's not, you know, it opened my eyes because I took him to one of his own.[38]

Breitbart writes: "Sherrod's racist tale is received by the NAACP audience with nodding approval and murmurs of recognition and agreement."[39] Condemnation of Sherrod's speech filled the airwaves, and she was condemned from nearly all sides, including the NAACP. The Obama administration forced her to resign. After she resigned, it emerged that her

---

[38] See http://en.wikipedia.org/wiki/Resignation_of_Shirley_Sherrod
[39] See http://mediamatters.org/research/201007220004

remarks had been taken drastically out of context: she told the anecdote quoted above in order to explain how wrong she was about race at the beginning of her career, and that she came to realize quickly that fighting for the poor was more important than race. Once this emerged, and the white farmers from the anecdote rose to Sherrod's defence, describing how she saved their farm and became their lifelong friend, Sherrod was offered a new government job.

If we assume that Breitbart was aware of the full context of Sherrod's speech, what he did was clearly utterly reprehensible. But was it a lie? The quotation of Sherrod was not a lie: she did utter the words that he quoted her as saying. And this will be true for all out of context quotations. They will, however, be highly deceptive. But the fact that out of context quotations are not lies does nothing at all to mitigate their wrongfulness, on my view. I think this is an important strength of the view that I take on the ethics of the lying–misleading distinction. (Breitbart's own words, however, may well be a lie: if he knows that Sherrod's audience was not actually approving of "Sherrod's racist tale", then he was lying.)

10 Other uses of 'saying'

Interestingly, it seems as though the notion of saying we have arrived at through examining the lying–misleading distinction plays other important roles in our lives as speakers. Even when lying and misleading are not at issue, speakers are sometimes very careful to convey something without saying it. And the same notion of saying seems to be involved in such manoeuvres, as we'll see below. Here's my preliminary take on why this notion of saying should have broader applicability: there are a variety of reasons that it may be considered problematic to say something. One of these, the one that does so much work in most of our discussion so far, is that it is something one believes to be false. But other reasons are possible as well: it might be rude to say it, or socially/politically unacceptable, or against government policy. When something is problematic to say for any of these reasons, but we want to communicate it anyway, we will often carefully construct our utterance to avoid saying it. And when we do this, it seems, we use what appears to be the same sort of conception of saying that we use when we carefully try to avoid lying.[40] I offer some examples of this below. (I don't take the examples to show conclusively that it's the same conception of saying, as that would require at the very least a much fuller range of examples than I've used. I merely take them to be suggestive.)

10.1 Doing something in the neighbourhood

Take, for example, an utterance from Hillary Clinton supporter and founder of Black Entertainment Television, Robert Johnson, made during her primary campaign against Barack Obama.

> I am frankly insulted that the Obama campaign would imply that we are so stupid that we would think Hillary and Bill Clinton, who have been deeply and emotionally involved in black issues since Barack Obama was doing something in the neighborhood—and I won't say what he was doing, but he said it in the book . . .[41]

It was obvious to everyone what Johnson meant by the phrase 'doing something in the neighborhood'; Johnson had in mind Obama's cocaine use. This is clear from his stated reluctance to 'say what [Obama] was doing', and the reference to Obama saying it in his book. (It's well known that Obama discussed his youthful cocaine use in his autobiography.) Importantly, Johnson conveyed but did not say that Obama used cocaine—even though it was true. This allowed him to maintain his defence of himself that he was merely thinking of Obama's work as a community organizer. And this is the result we get with our understanding of saying. On our understanding of saying, there is no room for the thought that Jonhson *said* anything at all about cocaine use. On Unconstrained understandings of saying, Johnson would count as saying that Obama was busy doing drugs while the Clintons were fighting for civil rights. To see this, consider Cappelen and Lepore's criterion for being said: a reasonable person might certainly report Johnson as having said that Obama was doing drugs while the Clintons were fighting for civil rights. On that account, then, Johnson has said this. The notion involved in the claim that Johnson carefully phrased his utterance so as not to say this cannot, then, be an Unconstrained one.

---

[40] Why we do this is another interesting matter. One reason may be simply deniability—if we haven't explicitly said something we can always insist that we didn't mean it. But a full discussion of these issues would take us too far off topic.

[41] From www.talkingpointsmemo.com/archives/063536.php (consulted 17 July 2009).

Why speak so carefully if he's not trying to deceive? The answer is, it seems to me, two-fold: first, it had already been made clear that explicit references to Obama's drug use are considered unacceptable (a state campaign chair for Clinton had been forced to resign over this issue). Second, Johnson gained deniability; and he used it. Responding to criticisms, he said:

> My comments today were referring to Barack Obama's time spent as a community organizer, and nothing else. Any other suggestion is simply irresponsible and incorrect.[42]

Johnson, then, had good reason to be very careful about what he said. Through most of this book, we have focused from the cases where this reason is due to an attempt at deception. But it needn't be, and this case begins to show that.

10.2 Politicians, marriages, and children

The Johnson case above is one that Constrained theories of saying can also cope with quite well: there isn't really room for any Expansion or Completion that would include Obama's cocaine use. But it doesn't require very much imagination to generate a case that shows Constrained notions of saying also fare poorly with this sort of careful wording. Imagine that a candidate for political office, P, had children prior to getting married. Imagine also a culture in which it would be considered dirty politics for an opponent to draw attention to this, but in which it is also clear that widespread knowledge of the fact would hurt P. It seems perfectly plausible that in this situation P's opponent might utter a sentence like (9), and when criticized explain it with (10).

(9)   P had children and got married.
(10) I didn't say *anything* about the order in which these events took place.

What would we make of this? I think it's pretty clear that we would think (10) is true—which fits very well with my account of saying and not so well with Constrained ones.[43] It's also clear, however, that we would judge the utterer, U, of (9) and (10) quite harshly. The fact that U did

---

[42] From www.cbsnews.com/blogs/2008/01/13/politics/fromtheroad/entry3706116.shtml (consulted 17 July 2009).

[43] Chapter 2 contains more detailed argumentation regarding a similar example and the options open to Constrained Theorists.

not *say* that the children preceded the marriage would not at all mitigate the "dirty politics" accusation. If anything, the careful wording in order to allow deniability would make U seem like an even slimier politician.

10.3 Letters of reference

Letters of reference also provide a rich resource for examples of this sort. Indeed, many versions of Grice's classic example work well. Suppose I am writing a reference for A, a terrible student, who is applying for a philosophy job. I write only "A is very punctual and always has a cheery smile". In doing this, I successfully (and truthfully) convey to the search committee that A is a very poor philosopher, but I do this without *saying* it. This, then, is another place where we see that the demand for very careful attention to what is said is not one limited to instances of deception.

10.4 Midwives and breastfeeding

In the United Kingdom, all normal pregnancies are handled by National Health Service (NHS) midwives, who also provide support and advice in the first weeks after a baby is born. NHS policy is that (unless there is some serious countervailing medical reason, like an infection that could be transmitted to the baby) midwives must always promote exclusive breast-feeding for the first six months. My midwife, observing my exhausted condition and desperate need to sleep, wanted to communicate to me that it might be alright to occasionally use formula—to engage in "mixed feeding". But, she felt, she could not say this. Instead, she said: "Here's an interesting fact. Did you know that most women in the Asian commu-nity do mixed feeding and their babies are just fine?" By doing this, she communicated to me that mixed feeding might be all right, without saying so. Clearly, she took this to be unacceptable to *say*—not because it was false, but because it would violate NHS policy for her to say it.[44]

10.5 Regime change as an objective

Jack Straw was Foreign Secretary of the UK when the second Iraq war was launched. Interviewed in 2010, he stated that:

---

[44] I have no idea whether she actually succeeded in not violating NHS policy. I doubt very much that the policy makes a sharp distinction between what midwives can say and what they can otherwise communicate. But clearly her desire to communicate the possibility of mixed feeling while not violating NHS policy is what led to her utterance.

as an objective, foreign regime chance was "improper and unlawful"... Yet asked whether that was Blair's view, Straw said only: "The prime minister was as well aware as I was that military action for regime change could not be an objective of British foreign policy."[45]

Straw had no intention of misleading. He avoided *saying* that Blair's objective was regime change, because that would be a very serious charge to make against him. But he is also avoiding *saying* that the prime minister did not have regime change as his objective, since (one supposes) that would be a lie. Instead, he opted to dodge the question. Did Straw mislead? This will probably depend on the audience one considers. I can imagine some audiences might have taken Straw to convey that Blair did not have regime change as an objective. However, more cynical audiences will not have been misled at all. Either way, though, Straw used his careful attention to what he *said* both to avoid lying and to avoid making a serious charge against Blair.

[45] *Guardian*, 22 January 2010, p. 4.

Conclusion

This book has argued for several claims. First, I argued for the importance of saying to the distinction between lying and merely misleading, one to which many assign moral significance. Next, I showed that none of the understandings of saying currently on the market can fulfil the role of saying in this distinction. This led directly into my search for an understanding of saying which could do this job. Once I'd sketched out what sort of understanding was needed, I turned to the ethical issues. There, I argued against the claim that lying was, all else being equal, morally worse than merely misleading. And yet, I suggested, this did not mean that we needed to abandon the idea that there is moral significance to this distinction. Decisions to lie or mislead can be very morally revealing, and this is what lends moral significance to the distinction. Finally, in the last chapter, I brought all this work together in the examination of a range of interesting cases.

But the main point of this book has not really been any of these specific claims. The main point of the book has been to suggest that issues like these—which bring together concerns and insights from both philosophy of language and ethics—are worth exploring. The ethicists who discuss the lying–misleading distinction have tended to give very little attention to the notion of saying that plays such a crucial role in the distinction. And the philosophers of language who work on saying (and related notions) have paid almost no attention to the lying–misleading distinction. Occasionally, an example involving a lie or a misleading will crop up—but without any sustained attention to the distinction and its complexities. I think this is a great shame, for these issues do connect up in important ways.

I also think that work like this can offer a new way forward in some entrenched debates in philosophy of language. As I noted at the outset, it is my suspicion that (many of) the various notions currently at use in the semantic–pragmatic distinction disputes should be viewed not as competitors, but as notions suited for different purposes. I have not attempted to establish this here (though I'd like to do that sometime). Instead, I have tried to demonstrate the usefulness of examining these notions by asking which is best suited to some particular purpose. My hope is that this book can serve as a kind of case study for this sort of investigation. I hope that it also serves to demonstrate the fruitfulness and interest of connecting issues in philosophy of language with issues in ethics, and even with an effort ot understand such things as events of significance in the real world.

References

Adler, Jonathan (1997) 'Lying, Deceiving, or Falsely Implicating', *Journal of Philosophy*, 94(9): 435–52.

—— [n.d.] 'Lying and Misleading: A Moral Difference', unpublished ms.

Almog, Joseph, Perry, John, and Wettstein, Howard (1989) *Themes from Kaplan*. Oxford: Oxford University Press.

Atkin, Albert (2006) 'There's No Place Like "Here" and No Time Like "Now"', *American Philosophical Quarterly*, 43(3): 271–80.

Bach, Kent (1992) 'Intentions and Demonstrations', *Analysis*, 52(3): 140–6.

—— (1994) 'Conversational Impliciture', *Mind and Language*, 9(2): 124–61.

—— (2001) 'You Don't Say?', *Synthese*, 128: 15–44.

—— (2002) 'Seemingly Semantic Intuitions'. In: *Meaning and Truth*, Keim J. Campbell, M. O'Rourke, and D. Shier (eds.) pp. 21–33. New York: Seven Bridges.

—— (2004) 'Minding the Gap'. In: *The Semantics/Pragmatics Distinction*, Claudia Bianchi (ed.), pp. 27–43. Stanford, CA: CSLI.

Borg, Emma (2004) *Minimal Semantics*. Oxford: Oxford University Press.

—— (2007) 'Minimalism versus Contextualism in Semantics'. In: *Context Sensitivity and Semantic Minimalism: Essays in Semantics and Pragmatics*, G. Preyer and G. Peter (eds.), pp. 546–71. Oxford: Oxford University Press.

Braun, David (2008) 'Indexicals', *Stanford Encyclopedia of Philosophy* (Fall edition), Edward N. Zalta (ed.), at: http://plato.stanford.edu/archives/fall2008/entries/indexicals

Brown, Penelope and Stephen C. Levinson (1987) *Politeness: Some Universals in Language Usage*. Cambridge: Cambridge University Press.

Calhoun, Cheshire (1989) 'Responsibility and Reproach', *Ethics*, 99(2): 389–406.

Camp, Elisabeth (2006) 'Contextualism, Metaphor, and What Is Said', *Mind and Language*, 21(3): 280–309.

Campbell, Keim J., M. O'Rourke, and D. Shier (2002) *Meaning and Truth*. New York: Seven Bridges, pp. 21–33.

Cappelen, Herman and E. Lepore (2005) *Insensitive Semantics*. Oxford: Blackwell.

Carson, Thomas (2006) 'The Definition of Lying', *Noûs*, 40(2): 284–306.

—— (2010) *Lying and Deception: Theory and Practice*. Oxford: Oxford University Press.

Carston, Robyn (1991) 'Implicature, Explicature and Truth-Theoretic Semantics'. In: *Pragmatics*, Steven Davis (ed.). New York: Oxford University Press.

—— (2002) *Thoughts and Utterances: The Pragmatics of Explicit Communication*. Oxford: Blackwell.

CBS News (1998) 'Tripp–Lewinsky Tapes 7', at: www.cbsnews.com/stories/ 1998/10/03/archive/main19029.shtml (consulted 13 August 2008).

Chisholm, Roderick and Thomas D. Feehan (1977) 'The Intent to Deceive', *Journal of Philosophy*, 74(3): 143–59.

Coleman, Linda and Paul Kay (1981) 'Prototype Semantics: The English Word *Lie*', *Language*, 57(1): 26–44.

Corazza, E., W. Fish, and J. Gorvett (2002) 'Who is I?', *Philosophical Studies*, 107(1): 1–21.

Davis, W. (1998) *Implicature: Intention, Convention, and Principle in the Failure of Gricean Theory*. Cambridge: Cambridge University Press.

—— (2005) 'Implicature', *Stanford Encyclopedia of Philosophy* (Summer edition), Edward N. Zalta (ed.), at: http://plato.stanford.edu/archives/sum2005/entries/ implicature

—— (2007) 'How Normative is Implicature?', *Journal of Pragmatics*, 39(10): 1655–72.

Fallis, Don (2009) 'What Is Lying?', *Journal of Philosophy*, 106(1): 29–56.

Frankfurt, Harry (2005) *On Bullshit*. Princeton, NJ: Princeton University Press.

Green, Stuart P. (2001) 'Lying, Misleading, and Falsely Denying: How Moral Concepts Inform the Law of Perjury, Fraud, and False Statements', *Hastings Law Journal*, 53: 157–212.

—— (2006) *Lying, Cheating, and Stealing: A Moral Theory of White-Collar Crime*. Oxford: Oxford University Press.

Grice, H. P. (1989) *Studies in the Way of Words*. Cambridge, MA: Harvard University Press.

Horn, L. (2010) 'WJ-40: Issues in the Investigation of Implicature'. In: *Meaning and Analysis*, Klaus Petrus (ed.), pp. 310–39. Basingstoke: Palgrave Macmillan.

Jonsen, Albert R. and Stephen Toulmin (1988) *The Abuse of Casuistry: A History of Moral Reasoning*. Los Angeles, CA: University of California Press.

Kamen, Al (2005) 'Ambigously anonymous', *Washington Post*, 19 October, A19, at: www.washingtonpost.com/wp-dyn/content/article/2005/10/18/AR2005101 801717.html (consulted 14 August 2008).

Kaplan, David (1989a) 'Demonstratives'. In: *Themes from Kaplan*, Almog *et al.* (eds.), pp. 481–563.

—— (1989b) 'Afterthoughts'. In: *Themes from Kaplan*, Almog *et al.* (eds.), pp. 565–614.

Keenan (Ochs), E. (1977) 'The Universality of Conversational Implicatures'. In: *Studies in Language Variation*, R. W. Fasold and R. W. Shuy (eds.). Washington, DC: Georgetown University Press.

King, Jeffrey C. and Jason Stanley (2005) 'Semantics, Pragmatics, and the Role of Semantic Content'. In: *Semantics versus Pragmatics*, Zoltan Gendler Szabo (ed.). Oxford: Oxford University Press.

MacIntyre, Alasdair (1994) 'Truthfulness, Lies, and Moral Philosophers: What Can We Learn from Mill and Kant?', *Tanner Lectures on Human Values*, pp. 309–69, delivered Princeton University, at: www.tannerlectures.utah.edu/lectures/documents/macintyre_1994.pdf (consulted 3 April 2012).

Mahon, James Edwin (2003) 'Kant on Lies, Candour and Reticence', *Kantian Review*, 7: 102–33.

—— (2008a) *International Journal of Applied Philosophy*, 22(2): 211–30.

—— (2008b) 'The Definition of Lying and Deception', *Stanford Encyclopedia of Philosophy* (Fall edition), Edward N. Zalta (ed.), at: http://plato.stanford.edu/archives/fall2008/entries/lying-definition

Meibauer, Jorg (2005) 'Lying and Falsely Implicating', *Journal of Pragmatics*, 37: 1373–99.

Michaelson, Eliot [n.d.] 'Lying and Content', unpublished ms.

Molloy, Cian (2009) 'Dublin Abuse Report Asks: "When Is a Lie Not a Lie?"', *National Catholic Reporter*, at: http://ncronline.org/news/accountability/dublin-abuse-report-asks-when-lie-not-lie (consulted 1 July 2010).

Morgan, J. L. (1978) 'Two Types of Convention in Indirect Speech Acts'. In: *Syntax and Semantics* Vol. 9: *Pragmatics*, P. Cole (ed.). New York: Academic Press.

Mustanski, Brian (2001) 'Semantic Heterogeneity in the Definition of "Having Sex"' for Homosexuals', unpublished ms.

Owens, David [n.d.] 'The Wrong of Untruthfulness', unpublished ms.

PBS (1998) 'President Bill Clinton', at: www.pbs.org/newshour/bb/white_house/jan-june98/clinton_1-21.html (consulted 14 August 2008).

Predelli, Stefano (1998) 'I Am Not Here Now', *Analysis*, 58: 107–12.

—— (2002) 'Intentions, Indexicals, and Communication', *Analysis*, 62: 310–15.

Récanati, François (1989) 'The Pragmatics of What Is Said', *Mind and Language*, 4(4): 295–329.

—— (2001) 'What Is Said', *Synthese*, 128(1–2): 75–91.

—— (2002) 'Unarticulated Constituents', *Linguistics and Philosophy*, 25(3): 299–345.

—— (2004) *Literal Meaning*. Cambridge: Cambridge University Press.

—— (2007) *Perspectival Thought: A Plea for (Moderate) Relativism*. Oxford: Oxford University Press.

Reimer, Marga (1991a) 'Demonstratives, Demonstrations, and Demonstrata', *Philosophical Studies*, 63: 187–202.

—— (1991b) 'Do Demonstrations Have Semantic Significance?' *Analysis*, 51: 177–83.

Romdenh-Romluc, Komarine (2002) 'Now the French Are Invading England!', *Analysis*, 62: 34–40.

—— (2006) 'I', *Philosophical Studies*, 128(2), 257–83.

Runciman, David (2006) 'Liars, Hypocrites and Crybabies', *London Review of Books*, 28: 21, at: www.lrb.co.uk/v28/n21/runc01_.html (consulted 14 August 2008).

Sanders, Stephanie A. and June Machover Reinisch (1999) 'Would You Say You "Had Sex" If . . . ', *Journal of the American Medical Association*, 281(3): 275–7.

Saul, Jennifer (2001) 'Critical Study of Davis, *Conversational Implicature*', *Noûs*, 35(4): 630–64.

—— (2002) 'Speaker Meaning, What Is Said, and What Is Implicated', *Noûs*, 36(2): 228–48.

—— (2010) 'Conversational Implicature, Speaker Meaning, and Calculability'. In: *Meaning and Analysis: New Essays on H. Paul Grice*, Klaus Petrus (ed.), pp. 170–83. New York: Palgrave Macmillan.

Searle, John (1978) 'Literal Meaning', *Erkenntnis*, 13: 207–24.

Soames, Scott (2002) *Beyond Rigidity: The Unfinished Semantic Agenda of Naming and Necessity*. New York: Oxford University Press.

—— (2005) 'Naming and Asserting'. In: *Semantics versus Pragmatics*, Zoltan Gendler Szabo (ed.). Oxford: Oxford University Press.

—— (2010) *Philosophy of Language*. Princeton, NJ: Princeton University Press.

Solan, Lawrence (2010) 'Lawyers as Insincere (But Truthful) Actors', ms, presented at Trust and Lying Workshop, Sheffield, UK.

Solan, Lawrence M. and Peter M. Tiersma (2005) *Speaking of Crime: The Language of Criminal Justice*. Chicago: University of Chicago Press.

Sorensen, Roy (2007) 'Bald-Faced Lies! Lying without the Intent to Deceive', *Pacific Philosophical Quarterly*, 88(2): 251–64.

—— (2011) 'What Lies behind Misspeaking', *American Philosophical Quarterly*, 48(4): 399–409.

Sperber, Dan and Deirdre Wilson (1986/1995) *Relevance*. Cambridge, MA and Oxford: Harvard University Press and Blackwell.

Stainton, Robert J. (2006) *Words and Thoughts: Subsentences, Ellipsis, and the Philosophy of Language*. Oxford: Oxford University Press.

Stanley, Jason (2000) 'Context and Logical Form', *Linguistics and Philosophy*, 23: 391–434. Oxford: Clarendon.

—— (2002) 'Making It Articulated', *Mind and Language*, 17(1–2): 149–68.

—— (2005) 'Semantics in Context'. In: *Contextualism in Philosophy*, Gerhard Preyer (ed.), pp. 221–54. Oxford: Oxford University Press.

Stanley, Jason and Zoltan Gendler Szabo (2000) 'On Quantifier Domain Restriction', *Mind and Language*, 15(2–3): 219–61.

Strudler, Alan (2010) 'The Distinctive Wrong in Lying', *Ethical Theory and Moral Practice*, 13: 171–9.

Taylor, Kenneth A. (2001) 'Sex, Breakfast, and Descriptus Interruptus', *Synthese*, 128: 45–61.

Travis, Charles (1996) 'Meaning's Role in Truth', *Mind*, 100: 451–66.

Velleman, J. David (2010) 'Regarding Doing Being Ordinary', paper presented at Trust and Lying Workshop, Sheffield, UK.

Wettstein, Howard (1984) 'How to Bridge the Gap Between Meaning and Reference', *Synthese*, 84: 63–84.

Williams, Bernard (2002) *Truth and Truthfulness: An Essay in Genealogy*. Princeton, NJ: Princeton University Press.

Wilmsen, David (2009) 'Understatement, Euphemism, and Circumlocution in Egyptian Arabic: Cooperation in Conversational Dissembling'. In: *Information Structure in Spoken Arabic*, Jonathan Owens and Alaa El Gibaly (eds.), pp. 243–59. London: Routledge.

Wintour, Patrick *et al.* (2010) 'Gordon Brown: Leadership Challenge was "Storm in a Teacup"', *Guardian*, 7 January, at: www.guardian.co.uk/politics/2010/jan/07/gordon-brown-immediate-general-election

Index